THE BOOK OF RUGS

PLATE I   KNOTTED WOOLEN CARPET (FRAGMENT); NORTHWEST PERSIA, CA. 1600

The field is covered with three systems of scrolling stems, stylized blossoms, and vases. In between the larger objects are richly blossoming branches and cloud bands. Two systems of arabesques with blossoms make up the main border. This is the only vase carpet on a white background.

240 x 150 cm. (8 ft. 2 in. x 4 ft. 9 in.) Approx. 500 knots per sq. in. Österreichisches Museum für angewandte Kunst, Vienna.

THE BOOK OF RUGS

Oriental and European

by Ignace Schlosser

CROWN PUBLISHERS, INC.   NEW YORK

TRANSLATED FROM THE GERMAN,
DER SCHÖNE TEPPICH IN ORIENT UND OKZIDENT

© 1960 BY KEYSERSCHE VERLAGSBUCHHANDLUNG GMBH, HEIDELBERG
© 1963 BY CROWN PUBLISHERS, INC.
LIBRARY OF CONGRESS CATALOG CARD NUMBER: 62-11812
PRINTED IN THE UNITED STATES OF AMERICA

CONTENTS

COLOR PLATES

PREFACE

There is nowhere a beginning
Neither is there anywhere an end.
            (George R. Stewart, Shepp Rock)

The history of carpets spans more than two thousand years—from its beginnings in southern Siberia, via the golden age of the Safavid dynasty in the sixteenth and seventeenth centuries, to the carpets of today, whose designs are still governed by the popular tradition of the main carpet regions and by the Turkish and Persian Court manufactures. It is the aim of this volume to supply a reliable guide for the collector and the potential buyer. However, a complete catalogue of the Oriental carpet in its infinite variety would be impossible.

The surviving historical carpets are distributed throughout the world's museums from Boston to Leningrad, from Stockholm to Vienna and Istanbul, where comparatively few carpet-lovers can enjoy them. Until quite recently, even photographs of these treasures were chiefly confined to rare and expensive books, available in many cases only with great difficulty.

Illustrations of carpets from all over the world, some of them in color, have been gathered for these pages. Many of the great museums and carpet-dealers from England, Austria, and Germany have supplied photographs. All the trade examples are from the postwar stock of their owners, more than adequate proof that "old" rugs can still be bought. That many priceless old pieces should have suffered some damage in the course of the centuries is hardly surprising, but does not detract from their value as works of art.

The author, Dr. Ignaz Schlosser, was until recently director of the Österreichische Museum für angewandte Kunst in Vienna. The museum's carpet collection, which includes many pieces formerly in the possession of the Austrian Court, occupies a leading position. By dealing at some length with Eastern history, Dr. Schlosser has tried to give the reader, who may well be confused by similar patterns and motifs in carpets from widely separated areas, a background to events that have affected the art of the West scarcely less than that of Asia.

The designs of nineteenth and twentieth century carpets are still very largely governed by the golden age of the Eastern carpet in the sixteenth and seventeenth centuries. It was then that the principal carpet regions—Turkey, Persia, and the Caucasus—produced patterns which have remained basically unchanged to the present day. The historical section of the book is devoted mostly to this period. The influence of the period on nineteenth- and twentieth-century carpets can be studied in the illustrations in the second part of the book, which also includes Western carpets.

Not so very long ago, the art of the Eastern carpet appeared doomed. From the middle of the last century onward, the making of carpets was controlled by dealers anxious to satisfy European and American taste. Orders for every possible design were accepted, and the century-old indigenous patterns were arbitrarily combined or disregarded. Customers frequently demanded Turkish designs from Persia, Persian from Turkey, or Turkoman from India. In addition, the new and then still very inferior synthetic colors were often used in place of the old vegetable dyes made according to carefully guarded recipes. Fortunately, the Persian carpet industry of today, largely state-controlled, has successfully reversed this process. Modern Persian carpets are therefore given a special place in this catalogue.

Technique is of paramount importance in the textile arts—so much so, that technical details often provide the key to date, origin, and value. The material of pile, warp, and weft, the different types of knot, the number of knots per square inch, patterns, motifs, and types of loom have all been discussed here at considerable length with the help of illustrations. Other chapters contain information about the care and purchase of rugs, about ways of cleaning them and of preventing moths. The glossary lists the most important terms. But all special problems of attribution and dating—of interest to the expert rather than the comparative beginner, and in any case bound to remain very often a matter of pure conjecture—have been deliberately avoided to prevent confusion. A course has been traced from the beginnings to the present day, from historical archetypes to the standard designs we know. Many a carpet-owner may well recognize in some historical carpets the ancestors of the octagons and rosettes of his own rugs.

THE CARPETS OF THE EAST

HISTORICAL OUTLINE

The lands in which the Eastern carpet originated have had a long and eventful history. Again and again, foreign invaders conquered and destroyed them; sometimes the invaders founded new cities. These wars extended practically throughout the Middle East and southeastern Europe, from the western parts of Asia Minor and Egypt to Greece and as far north as Scythia. Within a single ten-year period Alexander the Great conquered almost the entire Near East, but his empire soon disintegrated. For the next 500 years, Persia, Asia Minor, Syria, and the Caucasus were ruled by Parthians, Greeks, and Romans.

From the third century B.C. onward, Persia was governed by the Sassanians, who stood firm against Rome for over 400 years. In 641, the Arabs temporarily put an end to the Persian Empire, and Turkestan, Palestine, Syria, Egypt, and Spain all came under Arab domination. After the eleventh century, apart from the Caliphs, Turkish princes of the Ghazni, Seljuk, and Khwarizm dynasties ruled certain regions of Persia.

Migrations beginning in the sixth century brought whole nomad tribes to eastern Iran, where they came into contact with a more highly evolved civilization. Toward the end of the eleventh century, Asia Minor also fell under Seljuk domination and for over 200 years remained under the overlordship of the Sultanate of Rum. A few carpets survive from this period.

The Crusades, compared to the Mongolian and Tatar invasions under Genghis Khan (1220), brought little disturbance to the Near East. The Ottoman Empire, originally confined to Asia Minor, soon began to spread westward. Adrianople was taken in 1367; twenty-

**PLATE II WOOLEN PRAYER RUG; TURKISH COURT MANUFACTURE,
16TH CENTURY**

The red field of the mihrab is filled with large flower-heads, flower-ing branches, and foliage; in the spandrels are gray arabesques. The main border stripe has flowers and rosettes flanked with saw-edged leaves; in the guard stripes, small rosettes. This prayer rug is the ancestor of the whole group of Anatolian prayer rugs.
183 x 117 cm. (6 ft. x 3 ft. 10 in.) Warp and weft silk. Sehna or Persian knot, 350 knots per sq. in. Österreichisches Museum für angewandte Kunst, Vienna.

two years later, the Serbs were decisively defeated at Kossovo. Persia was thus given a brief respite.

By the end of the century both empires had fallen to Timur, though the Ottoman dynasty recovered after his death and once more pursued its policy of conquest in Europe. The Eastern Roman Empire fell to the Turks in 1453 with the capture of Constantinople, and in the next century the Turks defeated Hungary; Egypt also became nominally a part of the Turkish Empire. Baghdad, though captured in 1534, did not become a part of the empire till a century later.

Persia, where the arts had flourished under the Sassanian dynasty, was also attacked, and Tabriz, the capital, repeatedly taken by the Turks. There the conflict was religious as well as dynastic, for the Ottomans were Sunnites, the Persian Shiites.

In the fifteenth century Asia Minor still led in the art of carpet-making. The sixteenth saw Persia become pre-eminent. In India, after Timur's death, the arts also went through a golden age, under the Moguls, which lasted some two centuries.

The Persian invasions of Greece, Alexander's conquests, the Arab advance as far as Spain, the migrations of Turkish tribes, the Crusades, and the Mongolian invasions under Genghis Khan and Timur all brought about a meeting of civilizations. Few and far between, like islands in time, were the periods of calm when the arts could flourish. But even when whole empires were destroyed, civilizations to some extent survived.

As to the technical aspect of the Oriental carpet, it must be borne in mind that the principal carpet regions—Asia Minor and Persia— are mountainous, dry, and thinly populated, chiefly by nomadic tribes engaged in animal husbandry. Sheep, goats, in Persia also camels, supply most of the materials. Only the border regions, which have more rain, are to some extent cultivated. There, all kinds of plants are grown, including cotton. Even silk, though mostly imported from the Far East, is produced on a small scale.

THE CARPET
FROM THE
PAZYRYK VALLEY

THE OLDEST CARPET KNOWN

The earliest known carpet was discovered in 1949 in a Scythian burial site at Pazyryk in the Altai region, about fifty miles from the Outer Mongolian border. The Scythians, a nomad tribe of Iranian origin, were influenced by both the Graeco-Roman and the Chinese civilizations.

The Pazyryk carpet, with a quatrefoil field design framed by a border of five stripes, of which the fourth and second assume rather more importance than the others, suggests a comparatively longer development that may well have begun elsewhere. The palace of Sennacherib (seventh century B.C.) in Nineveh had pavements decorated in a similar manner, the central field with an all-over pattern of intersecting circles being surrounded by a border of four stripes, with lotus flowers in the second and the fourth and small rosettes in the others. The quatrefoil pattern also appeared in the palace at Nineveh.

CA 500 B.C.

The burial sites in the Altai region are thought to date from about 500 B.C. Carpets were undoubtedly made in various important cultural centers of Hither Asia at that time, chiefly in Sardis, the Lydian capital and after 546 B.C. one of the seats of the Persian

PLATE III KNOTTED WOOLEN CARPET; TURKISH COURT
MANUFACTURE, 16TH CENTURY

The red ground is filled with a pattern of rosettes, leaves, and flowering branches. The small round medallion and the corner pieces contain flowers and cloud bands. Here, in contrast to Persian examples, the medallion is almost swamped by the all-over decoration.

728 x 419 cm. (23 ft. 10 in. x 13 ft. 9 in.) Warp and weft silk. Sehna or Persian knot, 200 knots per sq. in. Österreichisches Museum für angewandte Kunst, Vienna.

administration, and in Babylon, which was conquered by Cyrus in 538 B.C.

The carpet thus did not suddenly appear from nowhere, nor was it developed in imitation of animal skins. It is more likely that it evolved as a mobile substitute for mosaic. Excavations at Olynthus (Macedonia) have brought to light colored mosaics with mythological scenes and animals of every kind (fifth to fourth centuries B.C.). Why, then, should not a nomad prince have longed for similar decoration for his tent?

MOBILE FLOOR DECORATION

It makes little difference whether mosaics merely inspired the designs of carpets or whether carpets were altogether adaptations of mosaic. Even the discoveries at Pazyryk do not answer the question of first origins. But they do prove that the art of the knotted carpet was already highly evolved in pre-Christian times.

Fig. 1   Detail of the five-stripe border of the Pazyryk carpet.

CTESIPHON
THE SPRING OF
CHOSROES

Carpets are often mentioned in the literature of Greek and Roman Antiquity. There is unfortunately no reference to technique, and we therefore do not know whether they were woven or knotted.

The next finds after the Pazyryk carpet (*ca.* 500 B.C.) were small fragments dating from between the third and sixth centuries A.D., from burial sites at Lou-Lan in Eastern Turkestan. They are too small—a piece with a blue lozenge design filled with red and blue dots, and the remains of a running dog border in brown and bluish-green—to permit any conclusions. In 637, Ctesiphon, the Sassanian capital, was conquered by the Arabs, and the famous "Spring of Chosroes," named after Chosroes I (531–79), fell into the victors' hands. Everything suggests that this was neither a carpet nor even a textile of any kind. The description speaks of "a wide border with flower beds, the flowers in blue, red, yellow, and white, and green stones. The yellow of the earth was imitated in gold, the water in crystal, the pebbles on the ground in pearls. Stems and branches were of gold and silver, leaves of silk, and fruits of colored stones." Apparently, the Spring of Chosroes was broken up later and a part sold for 20,000 dirhems. No carpet fragment could have had such

NEXT DISCOVERIES, 3RD TO 6TH CENTURIES A.D.

CTESIPHON

19

an outstanding—if indeed any—market value in the seventh century A.D.

But Arab references to carpets became more numerous. The floor of Harun al-Rashid's palace in Baghdad, in the second half of the eighth century, was said to have been covered with 22,000 carpets.

FARS, QAINATE, AZERBAIJAN   In the ninth century carpets were made at Fars (southwestern Persia); in the tenth the highlands of Qainat (northeastern Persia) were renowned for carpets and prayer rugs, and contemporary records speak of carpet-weavers in Azerbaijan (northwestern Persia) in approximately the year 1200.

Genghis Khan's invasions at the beginning of the thirteenth century, and those of his grandson Hulagu Khan about fifty years later, probably stopped production for a while. But the later Mongol Khans were men of considerable culture. When Ghazan Khan built his new palace at the outskirts of Tabriz, the floors were covered with carpets from Fars.

ANATOLIA
(Asia Minor)

From the thirteenth century onward, the number of surviving carpets and pictorial records increases. Several early examples from the mosques of Ala-ad-Din in Konya and Eshrefoglu in Beyshehir belong to the Seljuk period (*Ills. 2 and 3*). Like some other thirteenth-century pieces, they have wide calligraphic (Kufic) or panel borders which contrast with the all-over design of the field. This impression of an endless pattern is increased by the diagonal arrangement, the connecting links from row to row, and the apparent lack of relationship between field and border.

Italy's close contacts with the Near East led to the importation of Anatolian rugs. That these were greatly treasured by their owners is obvious from the work of Italian—and later also Northern—painters from the fourteenth century onward. At first, we find designs of stylized animals within large squares, though it would hardly be safe to treat these early pictures as scientific records.

Two rugs, one in Stockholm and one in Berlin (*Ills. 4 and 5*), are more reliable evidence. The completely rigid animal forms are clearly taken from some other technique; above all, they must have belonged to a much higher civilization before their descent into folk art.

13TH CENTURY: KONYA, BEYSHEHIR

BROAD BORDERS WITH CALLIGRAPHIC DESIGN

CARPETS IN PAINTINGS

15TH CENTURY
ORNAMENTAL PATTERNS

Another type of design in Anatolian fifteenth-century rugs is based on purely geometric principles, the field being divided either into large octagons filled with geometric motifs (*Ill.* 9) or into a pattern of small polygons (*Ills. 6 to* 8). The outlines of these small polygons and the dividing lines between rows can be interlaced in different ways. The border, originally a succession of Kufic characters, is transformed into an elaborate network. Islamic architecture already used calligraphy for its decorative qualities; mihrabs and doorways frequently bore inscriptions, particularly in the fourteenth century. Persian fifteenth-century carpets were created on very similar principles, and we can safely assume a general impulse toward geometric design throughout the carpet regions of the Middle East.

PLANT MOTIFS AND
ARABESQUES
16TH CENTURY

In the sixteenth century this world of rigid and stylized forms came under the influence of the Persian enthusiasm for plant motifs and related ornaments, such as the arabesque. In 1516, Tabriz, the capital of Azerbaijan and the residence of the Shah, was conquered by the Turks, who carried off many leading craftsmen on that occasion and throughout the following decades. A series of surviving carpets from this period (*Ills. 14 to 21, Pl.* II) bears witness to the skill of the Persian carpet-masters and their pupils. Their work shares certain characteristics, such as the nobly outlined and detailed

PERSIAN CARPET-MASTERS
IN ANATOLIA
FLORAL ELEMENTS

plant forms, the use of "Turkish" flowers like tulips, carnations, and hyacinths with Persian stylized giant flower-heads and foliage, the absence of animals or the human form (though some floral elements show a certain playful or perhaps ironic resemblance to animals),

PERSIAN KNOT

the simplified border with identical or very similar guard stripes (*Ills. 14, 15*), and the use of the Persian knot. In the finest examples, warp and weft are of silk.

CONSTANTINOPLE, USHAK

How close a connection there was with this Court manufacture, based in all probability on Constantinople and Ushak, is hard to tell. That it existed is certain, because many characteristic Ushak details are also found in carpets of Turkish Court manufacture (*Ills. 10, 16*). Ushak was undoubtedly an important center which

Fig. 2 *Cloud band motif, from the border of a carpet of Turkish Court manufacture*

produced some very large carpets and a variety of designs (*Ills.* 10 to 13). Even in large medallions the field design is treated like a section of an all-over pattern. A second medallion system is usually developed along the edge (*Ill.* 10), leaving very little of the dark ground, which is generally covered with scrolling stems. Sometimes the medallions seem frozen into rigidity (*Ill.* 11); sometimes, reduced to small polygonal fields. Again, the field may be covered with a network of angular arabesques, often yellow and red, in the manner of an all-over design. The principal colors of Ushak carpets are usually red, blue, and yellow or ivory; others play only a very subordinate part. The borders are vaguely Persian, though somewhat simplified. At the narrow ends, the design is often horizontally distorted. Occasionally, like a faint memory of the past, there are interlacement borders reminiscent of Arabic letters (*Ills. 5 and 6*). In many seventeenth- and eighteenth-century rugs the term "Anatolian," without any further specification, has to suffice.

TRIAD: RED, BLUE, YELLOW

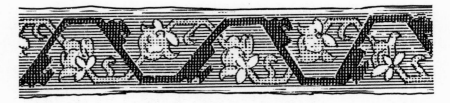

Fig. 3 *Scroll border (double wavy shoots)*

Fig. 4 *Arabesque border*

Fig. 5 *Kufic border*

The principal field designs are:

An arrangement of spheres and cloud bands (the *Chintamani* pattern, *Ill.* 22).

The so-called bird motif, a design of angular stylized leaves, suggestive of birds (*Ill.* 23).

Vases and fragments of scrolling stems (*Ill.* 26).

The field of the mihrab (in prayer rugs) either left bare (*Ill.* 24) or divided by columns (*Ills.* 25, 27).

The principal border themes are:

Scrolling stems, or tendrils, with cloud bands (*Fig.* 7).

Scrolling stems with rosettes.

Angular arabesques.

Panels with geometric designs, usually some rudimentary motif (*Fig.* 8).

Wide arabesque bands with toothed or saw-edged outline (*Fig.* 9).

Reciprocal trefoils on a light ground.

The memory of Persia, however distant, is always there. Turkey's trade with Europe remained brisk until well into the eighteenth century. At one time, the frontiers of the Turkish Empire were only a few miles outside Vienna. Even in the early nineteenth century, Oriental carpets were always described as "Turkey," just as in the more recent past they have collectively been known as "Persian."

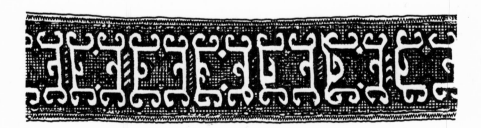

Fig. 6 *Kufic border*

25

Geographical names, whether those of the place of production or of trade centers, have been associated with Anatolian carpets to any considerable degree only since the last century, chiefly with certain types of prayer rug such as Ghiordes, Kula, Ladik, Madjur, and some others.

EXPORT TO EUROPE

Turkey's close though by no means always peaceful contact with the West meant that the supply of Turkish carpets to Europe never ceased, especially as Smyrna and the district around also could produce very large pieces, thus continuing the tradition of Ushak.

SMYRNA

The colors of the Smyrna carpet—still called "Turkey" in England—are chiefly red, green, and blue. Since the pile is very long, the pattern usually appears somewhat blurred. There is a preference for medallions of all sizes, and for medallion systems, with the corner pieces sometimes joined like curtains.

HEREKE

Among other examples designed with an eye to the European market are the carpets made in the Sultan's Court workshops at Hereke in the nineteenth century. Apart from copies of seventeenth-century patterns, there are some exceptionally fine pieces entirely European in character (*Ill. 112*). Hereke also produced knotted silk rugs (*Ill. 113*).

THE ANATOLIAN PRAYER RUG

But the principal Anatolian contribution is the small rug made by the independent craftsman working in his own home. The most important among these is the prayer rug. Its main feature, the prayer arch or mihrab, is borrowed from the mosque, but the character of its design varies from place to place. Some mihrabs are supported by pillars, which may dissolve into floral stripes. The field of the mihrab is usually empty, though it sometimes contains flowers and flowering branches, or a lamp, a vessel, or a branch suspended from the arch. There is generally a cross panel above and below the mihrab, the whole being enclosed within a border frequently reminiscent of some of the Classic borders of the sixteenth century, though the patterns are usually broken up (*Figs. 10, 11, 12, 13*). Apart from the usual border arrangement—a wide principal border

Fig. 7 Scrolls, used with cloud bands

Fig. 8 Panels with geometric designs, from the border of a seventeenth-century Transylvanian carpet

Fig. 9 Wide arabesque band, from the border of an eighteenth-century Transylvanian carpet

27

Fig. 10 *A border with large blossoms and paired leaves, from a seventeenth century Anatolian carpet.*

Fig. 12 *Tulips and carnations, from the border of an eighteenth-century prayer rug*

stripe and narrow guard stripes—there are multiple borders of narrow stripes. In the East these are called *shobokli,* a term derived from the Turkish word for pipestem; they may contain carnations, hyacinths, or tulips, often stylized beyond recognition.

GHIORDES Ghiordes, the Gordium of Antiquity, has preserved the Classic tradition of the Anatolian prayer rug more faithfully than any other region (*Ill. 114*). The mihrab, at first curved, later became steep and pointed. It is frequently supported by piers or pillars. Scrolling stems with large flowers, or small branches, each with three fruits or flowers, fill the border, the spandrels, and the cross panel which **KIS-GHIORDES** is usually above the mihrab. In the Kis-Ghiordes, a rug given to or woven by young girls in the East as part of their dowry, a favorite design is a small central medallion with medallion quarters within a border of reciprocal triangles divided by a broad white band (*Ill. 26*).

Another very common type of Anatolian rug, generally of a more

Fig. 11   Ghiordes border, ca. *1800*

Fig. 13   Angular scrolls between narrow guard stripes, from the border of an eighteenth-century Anatolian carpet

vigorous character, was made at Kula. Since the red has usually faded, the general impression is of blues and yellows. In these, there is a cross panel only above the mihrab, which is slightly flatter than in Ghiordes rugs. Spandrel, cross panel, and border—generally of many narrow stripes (shobokli)—are usually covered with stars and little flowers. In the so-called Cemetery Kula (*Ill. 115*), the field of the mihrab contains a landscape motif often interpreted as a tomb. These rugs used at cemeteries and at funerals are by no means confined to Kula. Ghiordes and Kula rugs are made in districts not very far apart. Though they are different in many respects, they share so many features that attribution, as with many other Anatolian rugs, is not always easy.

The prayer rugs of Ladik, the Laodica of Antiquity, also go back to the seventeenth and eighteenth centuries. In early examples, the mihrab used to contain six or eight pillars (*Ill. 14*). Later these were omitted, though the tripartite gable was retained for some time. The gables of later Ladik rugs are crow-stepped, often with elaborate

KULA

CEMETERY KULA

LADIK

29

lamps hanging down from the center. The cross panel, at first above the mihrab and later below, is usually filled with rows of long-stemmed tulips (*Ill. 116*). In earlier pieces, the spandrels contained broad leaves or a row of pointed arabesques reminiscent of battlements (*Zinnenmuster* in German; i.e., "battlement motif"). These motifs gradually withered, to be replaced in the border by geometric panels, increasingly angular scrolls, and pointed arabesques, which later acquired comblike wings.

MUDJUR — In the rugs of Mudjur, in Central Anatolia, the mihrab is crow-stepped and outlined in several colors, with a small finial (*Ill. 117*). The field contains a small tree almost bereft of leaves, or is altogether empty. The cross panel appears above the mihrab. Rosettes within squares form the principal border stripe.

KIRSHEHIR — The rugs of nearby Kirshehir are sometimes known as Sultan. The crow-stepped mihrab is occasionally outlined in even more colors (*Ill. 118*). The cross panel, either above or below the mihrab, is filled with arabesques outlined with hooks. Detached flowers or small branches form the border, which may consist of many stripes.

MILAS — Another important center is Milas, south of Smyrna, near the Mediterranean coast. An outstanding feature of the Milas prayer rug is the lozenge-shaped mihrab (*Ill. 120*). The field may contain a tree or a small medallion, or it may be empty. The space above the mihrab is filled with the large stylized leaves characteristic of seventeenth- and eighteenth-century Anatolian rugs. The principal border stripe, of five or seven smaller stripes, contains large flowerheads, leaves, and scrolling stems. Except in prayer rugs, the field is divided into narrow vertical stripes of small floral motifs and S-forms, or angular scrolls. The border is then very narrow, with small rosettes or scrolls.

MAKRI OR RHODES — Makri rugs, though supposedly in no way connected with the island, are also known as "Rhodes" (*Ill. 119*). The field is frequently divided into two or three elongated hexagons of different colors, filled with all kinds of geometric or highly stylized designs.

The border stripes, usually three or four in number and of approximately the same width, contain rosettes, angular scrolls, and S-forms.

KONYA

Konya, the Iconicum of Antiquity, already played an important role in the history of the Anatolian carpet in Seljuk days. The mihrab is wide, with a comparatively flat crow-stepped gable; the field contains flowers growing from the base. The flowers in the spandrels and the scrolls in the border are stylized in the extreme.

ANATOLIA

Anatolia, the Turkish name of Asia Minor, means "Land of the Rising Sun." (In England and America, the term "Anatolian" is used collectively for the rugs of Asia Minor; in German-speaking countries it is confined to rugs that cannot be further classified.) The Anatolian design is usually geometric, with rarely any trace of even the most stylized floral motifs. Right angles predominate (*Ill. 121*), and borders often consist of one broad stripe, the subsidiary border stripes having been reduced to thin lines.

TUZLA

The village of Tuzla is situated on the lake of Tuz Gul, in the province of Konya. In Tuzla prayer rugs, the mihrab is crow-stepped, and has a small finial as in the rugs of Mudjur. The field is decorated with a floral design (*Ill. 122*). Within the fairly large cross panel is an octagon enclosing a star formed by small, long-stemmed flowers. The multiple border includes zigzag forms, angular scrolls, and rosettes.

KAISARIIEH

Kaisariieh, the Biblical Caesarea, at one time produced silk rugs. The prayer rugs of the region resemble those of Ghiordes.

YURUK

The Yuruks, a Kurdish nomad tribe, once roamed western Anatolia. Their rugs are a reflection of their travels. The field is usually covered with diagonal stripes patterned with small geometric motifs, severely stylized cypresses, or a row of lozenge-shaped medallions and a wealth of hook motifs. A typical Yuruk border consists of a succession of small lozenges, of which every other sports four hooks (*Ill. 123*).

BERGAMA

The few prayer rugs of Bergama in western Anatolia, the classic Pergamos, are of no set type. Bergama rugs are almost square (*Ill.*

124). A favorite theme is a medallion, in shape something halfway between a cross and a polygon. This medallion, like the rest of the field, is covered with small motifs, some of which resemble plants, others animals. It almost seems as if the Turkish tradition of the time before the adoption of Persian design was continued in the rugs of Bergama. A darker variety, chiefly in somber reds and blues, is known as Yakshibehdir.

YAKSHIBEHDIR

SAPHS

Saphs, or family prayer rugs with a series of mihrabs, were produced in several districts of Anatolia. They have all the characteristic border and field designs of their particular group.

TYPICAL CHARACTERISTICS
OF ANATOLIAN RUGS

Most Anatolian rugs consist entirely of wool. Cotton, for warp and weft or for pure white, is very rarely used. The colors are generally bright and varied, though their range is not quite so wide or subtle as in Persian rugs. Red, blue, yellow, green, ivory, and white are the favorites, and the warp and weft threads are often dyed the predominating color of the pile. The Ghiordes or Turkish knot is employed. Both in early and nineteenth-century examples, the weft is not always taken across the entire warp after each row. We cannot tell whether this happened because someone was working very fast, or because a new pattern was being tried out. The resultant triangle, and the diagonal joins to the neighboring sections, can be clearly seen from the back.

KILIMS

In some districts of Anatolia, kilims or smooth-faced, pileless carpets assumed considerable importance. For a short while all smooth-surfaced carpets were called Karamanies, after the leading center of production and distribution in the East. A kilim (the word means, literally, a woven fabric) is reversible, comparatively fine, and rather thin. In their country of origin kilims are also used to cover carts.

PLATE IV   THE VIENNA HUNTING CARPET (SILK); PERSIAN COURT
MANUFACTURE, SECOND HALF 16TH CENTURY

Within the eight-pointed green medallion (not shown) and the
corner pieces are dragons and phoenixes; in the ruby border are genii
among clouds, birds, and flowering scrolls. The hunting scenes are
confined to the orange field, where huntsmen, both mounted and on
foot, are pursuing every kind of animal. Flowers and flowering
shrubs indicate the landscape. The whole carpet is lavishly brocaded
in gold and silver. This is one of the most famous carpets in existence,
a true Court product in the choice of subject, material, and technique
no less than in its colors and the delicate drawing.
693 x 323 cm. (22 ft. 9 in. x 10 ft. 7 in.) Approx. 740–750 knots per sq. in.
Österreichisches Museum für angewandte Kunst, Vienna.

EGYPT

In trying to discover anything about carpets in medieval Egypt, we are more or less confined to literary sources. Some fragments of the textiles that were used as floor coverings, with the loops formed by the weft threads cut open, survive from the time between the eighth and tenth centuries. There is frequent mention of carpets in the Fatimite period (tenth to twelfth century). The Caliph Al-Amir (1101–30) is said to have carpeted his audience chamber with silk in summer and wool in winter. Whether these carpets were woven or knotted is not mentioned. Again, there are records that Spanish carpets were used at the Fatimid court in 1124. It is also likely that Anatolian carpets reached Egypt, since there was brisk and constant trading throughout the Mediterranean region.

The impetus to an Egyptian carpet industry did not come through the political links between the Mamelukes and the rulers of fourteenth-century Anatolia, but through the connection with Timur's son, Shah Rukh, who greatly encouraged Persian art and culture in his capital, Herat, and through his successor, Usun Hasan. Persian craftsmen probably came to Egypt under their reign.

A number of carpets can be attributed to the period between the end of the fifteenth and the middle of the sixteenth century. The characteristics of this group (*Ills. 95, 96, 98*), are as follows:

    Geometric designs predominate.

    The center medallion, a star developed out of an octagon, is extended by small geometric forms as far as the border. If the carpet is very long, stripes with geometric or floral designs are added.

Floral motifs are always very small. The leaves are either mushroom-shaped on thin stems, or lanceolate. The finer the carpet (*Ills. 96 and 98*), the more the pattern resembles a mosaic ("mosaic pavement").

The principal border stripe is either divided into panels of various size, or filled with small scrolling stems.

The predominating colors are green, red, and blue.

The Sehna or Persian knot is used.

CHANGE OF DECORATION
UNDER THE TURKS

More Persian craftsmen probably came to Cairo with the Turkish conquest of Egypt in 1517. They had been captured when the Turks occupied Tabriz three years earlier. Their arrival did not at once change the designs of Egyptian carpets, though more modern forms, chiefly naturalistic flowers—carnations, tulips, hyacinths—leaves, and arabesques, did eventually prevail. The basic colors remained the same, but red rather than green came to predominate.

In 1585, Sultan Murad III wrote to the Governor of Egypt demanding eleven carpet-masters and a quantity of wool (about 3,500 lbs.). The eleven men were sent to the Turkish capital—they may even have gone of their own choice. But their store of wool would certainly have been inadequate to set up a Court manufacture. At most, it might have been enough for fifteen to twenty medium-sized carpets (today, home-workers in some districts of Persia are allowed 8 lbs. of knotting wool per sq. yd. and 3 lbs. of cotton for warp and weft).

The transfer of the carpet-masters did not result in an Ottoman Court manufacture, nor did it cause irreparable damage to Egyptian carpet production. Nevertheless, there is no evidence of an Egyptian carpet art after the seventeenth century.

PERSIA

Our knowledge of Persian carpets in the fifteenth century is based on Persian miniatures; in the carpets of this period there is a close REPRESENTATION IN PERSIAN MINIATURES resemblance to the geometric designs of Anatolian carpets. Of earlier Persian carpets, we know from travelers' reports only that they were greatly inferior to the products of Anatolia.

The carpets in early miniatures show the field divided into squares, outlined by interlacement forms. Occasionally, lines are ordered into geometric designs, or treated more freely as small scrolling stems. There are usually Kufic borders, as in Anatolian rugs.

At the end of the fifteenth century, altogether different carpets suddenly appeared in Persian miniatures: the field now covered with a medallion and scrolls, and scrolls also forming the principal motif of the border. Many types of Persian carpet have retained this kind of decoration to the present day. It is not certain in which realm of the applied arts—the miniature, bookbinding, or the carpet—these forms originated.

Like the development of painting, sculpture, and architecture in the Italian Renaissance, the history of the Persian carpet is closely connected with the ruling house. The Safavid dynasty was founded SAFAVID DYNASTY by Ismail I in 1499. Ismail was followed in 1524 by Shah Tahmasp; the years between 1587 and 1629 saw the reign of Shah Abbas the

35

Great, who was succeeded in turn by Safi and Abbas II.

With the consolidation of the dynasty, standards rose. Commissions became more numerous and factories were set up to meet the demands of the Court. The close co-operation between artists, craftsmen, and patrons made the sixteenth and seventeenth centuries a gold age whose triumphs in the art of the carpet have never been repeated. The carpet ceased to be mere floor covering and was restored to the rank of a work of art in its own right.

Some of the most important innovations in the designs of carpets of Persian Court manufacture (*Ills. 29 to 55*) are these: Border and field stand in a well-balanced relationship. The border, which has become a frame in the true sense, consists of a broad stripe with a continuous motif and narrow guard stripes. The corners are carefully worked out, not left to chance. The field design no longer appears like a section of an all-over pattern, but is oriented toward a vertical and a horizontal axis. Medallion carpets have quarter medallions at the corners. These differ sometimes from the center medallion, so that any suggestion of an all-over pattern is avoided.

Large center medallions (*Ills. 29 to 41*) enjoyed great popularity, but hardly two of them are alike. This type of decoration was probably inspired by the design of domes. If we imagine ourselves standing under a dome, which is projected to the area below, on top of an existing pattern, we can see how the medallion in carpets of this type introduces a second layer of decoration, which often portrays scenes belonging to an entirely different realm. This characteristic is particularly obvious in the carpet shown in *Ill. 40,* though there are other examples.

Thus, the carpet in the Museo Poldi Pezzoli in Milan (*Ill. 30*) contains hunting scenes in the field, but birds and clouds in the medallion. In the Vienna Hunting Carpet (*Pl.* IV), the field is filled with hunting scenes, the medallion with heavenly dragons and phoenixes. In the carpet in the Clarence Mackay Collection (*Ill.* 32), there are again clouds and birds in the medallion, whereas

GOLDEN AGE OF ORIENTAL
RUGS IN THE 16TH AND
17TH CENTURIES

MOST IMPORTANT
INNOVATIONS
RELATION BETWEEN BORDER
AND FIELD DESIGN

LARGE CENTER MEDALLION

CHARACTERISTIC EXAMPLES

Fig. 14   Palmette border, from a Persian carpet

Fig. 15   Cloud-band border, from a Persian carpet

the field is a landscape with cypresses and flowering trees and animals of every kind. The medallion in the carpet in the collection of Prince Schwarzenberg (*Ill.* 38) is developed as an enclosed garden with winding paths and a duckpond; wild animals disport themselves amid cypresses and other trees in the rest of the field.

Because of the elongated shape of these carpets, pendants are frequently added to the medallion (*Ills.* 29 *to* 33, 39); these may be rectangular, lobed, or have a variety of other forms.

Photographs of famous carpets of this outstanding period show us that no two examples are the same, or even display recurring types of border or field design. Every one of them is an individual work of art.

INDIVIDUAL WORKS OF ART

37

NATURALISTIC DESIGNS

But the large medallion is only one of many types of decoration. Sometimes the top layer of the composition consists of a series of small medallions or cartouches forming a regular pattern (*Ill. 40, Pl. V*). Naturalistic landscapes, flowers (*Ills. 31, 32, 36, 38, 39, 48, 63, 64*), animals (*Ills. 44, 47, 50*), hunting scenes (*Pl. IV*), and even gardens (*Ills. 61, 62*) complete with flower beds, and ponds with birds and fishes, also occur. The so-called vase carpets, with rich floral decoration, form a category of their own (*Ills. 55 to 58, Pl. I*). Their designs even influenced Caucasian carpets for some time. In other examples, the composition is dominated by large arabesques drawn in dark outlines and interspersed with cloud bands and flower-heads (*Ill. 65*).

FLOWERS, ORNAMENTS, ANIMALS

The flowers on Persian carpets vary greatly. Sometimes they are naturalistic (*Ill. 64*); more often, each blossom is an elaborate composition that dissolves into a wealth of ornate detail and is completely independent of nature or tradition (*Ill. 55 to 58*). When a flower grows rather large it is filled with smaller flowers. Leaves are treated similarly. The principal ornamental devices are the scrolling stem, the arabesque, and the cloud band, the last-named of Chinese origin (*Figs. 14 to 17*). All are found in an almost infinite variety. Hunting carpets include every kind of game and wild animal, as

Fig. 16   Cloud bands, from a sixteenth-century Persian vase carpet

well as—borrowed from Chinese art—dragons, phoenixes, and chilins (unicorns).

Silk is sometimes used, not only for warp and weft, but for the pile. But here we must distinguish between the finely knotted, silk carpets of the sixteenth century (*Ill. 35, Pl.* IV) and the so-called Polanaise rugs of the seventeenth (*Ills. 68 to 70, Pl.* VI). Some of

these rugs display the Polish arms; therefore the name. In 1601, Sigismund III (Sigismund Vasa), King of Poland, sent the Armenian merchant Muratovitz to Kashan to supervise the work on rugs ordered there. Rugs of this type were probably intended for Europe from the very first; this circumstance would account for the deterioration of craftsmanship, the widespread use of cotton for warp and weft, the low number of knots—approximately 190 to 250 per sq. in., compared with between 550 and 750 per sq. in. in the pure silk carpets of the sixteenth century—the lavish use of gold and silver brocading, and the not particularly detailed design with its distinctly "Baroque" traits. The same symptoms appear in Chinese export art.

The present system of local attribution has been based on the main carpet centers in the nineteenth century, many of which are of course much older. The principal areas are northwestern Persia (Tabriz, *Ills. 40, 45, 54, 56 to 59, 61 to 63*), central Persia (Kashan, Isfahan, Joshagan), southern Persia (Kerman), and eastern Persia (Herat, *Ills. 51 to 53*).

An exception must be made for carpets of Court manufacture, which differ in each case and cannot be fitted into any particular group.

The Shah's residence—the city was occupied three times, in 1514, 1533, and 1548—up to the first Turkish occupation, and again at intervals in the sixteenth century, was Tabriz. Shah Tahmasp resided at Kazvin, northwest of Teheran; Shah Abbas the Great chose Isfahan as his capital. It is known from the reports of early travelers that Isfahan had royal carpet workships in the vicinity of the palace. The moving of such a workshop along with the rest of the royal household could have presented little difficulty. Production could have been resumed within a short time, as long as designers and carpet-masters were available. Northwestern Persia seems to have been the leading center of every kind of carpet manufacture for a considerable time. Many of the favorite Persian designs appear in the rugs of the nearby Caucasus.

PERSIAN COURT
MANUFACTURE

It is because of these changes that the author prefers to describe the finest carpets of the sixteenth and early seventeenth centuries merely as "Persian Court manufacture," rather than to give too much importance to their place of origin. It is never easy to draw any conclusions from the distribution of certain types in the ninteenth century; some carpets have undergone many changes of attribution in the course of time. A typical produce of Court manufacture is the woven silk rug, whose pattern is derived from knotted carpets (*Ill. 72, Pl.* VII).

CULTURAL DECLINE IN THE
17TH CENTURY

The death of Shah Abbas in 1629 was followed by more wars with the Turks. Hamadan, Yerevan, Tabriz, and Baghdad, Persia's western and northern provinces, were lost, and after a century of decline the Safavid dynasty was overthrown by Afghan invaders. These wars affected the art of the carpet, which in consequence was probably confined to villages or to nomad tribes. Though village and nomad production had always existed, it had been completely overshadowed —at times undoubtedly also influenced—by the Court workshops in the sixteenth century. But too little survives of these years to allow any definite conclusions.

CHOICE OF PATTERNS

Gradually, the different regions of the Persian empire came to show a preference for certain designs, chiefly all-over patterns both large and small, the medallion (one center medallion or medallion rows), or naturalistic or stylized or geometric forms. Many districts did not confine themselves to one particular type.

More and more, urban workshop masters and villagers working to order began to comply with the demands of their customers,

On the red ground are rows of quatrefoil and trefoil medallions
within which are pairs of birds, arabesques, flowering scrolls, and
cloud bands. The space between the medallions is filled with flower-
and fruit-bearing trees. In the main border are stripe arabesques and
panels with flowering scrolls; more flowering scrolls appear on the
black ground.

540 x 270 cm. (17 ft. 9 in. x 8 ft. 10 in.) Approx. 170–180 knots per sq. in.
Österreichisches Museum für angewandte Kunst, Vienna.

PLATE V **BROCADED SILK RUG; PERSIAN COURT MANUFACTURE, FIRST HALF 17TH CENTURY**

The red field contains silver cloud bands and yellow flowering scrolls; the border, scrolling stems on a green ground.
214 x 141 cm. (7 ft. x 4 ft. 7 in.) Approx. 180 to 190 knots per sq. in.
Österreichisches Museum für angewandte Kunst, Vienna. Bequest of Clarice de Rothschild.

Fig. 17 Arabesques, from a sixteenth-century Persian carpet

many of whom were foreigners. The models were the carpets of the golden age of the sixteenth century. At the same time, the popular tradition, though changed by the influence of the Court workshops, was carried on by individual craftsmen and small employers. But here, too, the motifs were those of Court manufacture, though simplified, stylized, broken up, and distorted.

URBAN WORKSHOPS AND POPULAR TRADITION

Since the nineteenth century, the designs of Persian carpets have been based on the great tradition of the Safavid dynasty, by no means always with happy results. This applies particularly to the products of the great carpet centers of Tabriz, Kashan, Meshed, Kerman, and Isfahan, which have supplied the European and Persian market to the present day. The pandering to foreign taste has had its effect. Persian art schools turn out innumerable designers who, working chiefly in the Classic tradition, show a love of unrestrained ornament, fight shy of even the smallest empty space, and are also quite willing to absorb European "ideas."

PERSIAN CARPETS OF THE 19TH CENTURY

EUROPEAN INFLUENCE

Tabriz carpets have a very short pile, which makes the drawing stand out with great clarity. The Ghiordes or Turkish knot is used; warp and weft are cotton. A favorite motif is the medallion (*Ill. 126*).

TABRIZ

Fig. 18 Herati *pattern*

The Sehna or Persian knot is employed in the carpets of Kashan. The pile is short, the surface almost like velvet. Since knotted silk rugs are also made in Kashan, it is thought that the silk carpets of the Safavid dynasty may have come from there. The field is usually designed around a large medallion; the border consists chiefly of delicate scrolling stems (*Ill. 127*).

KASHAN

MESHED Meshed, the capital of Khurasan (northeastern Persia), is noted for its almost square rugs, with clear designs in pastel shades. Warp and weft are cotton, and the knotting is Sehna or Persian (*Ill. 128*).

KERMAN The carpets of Kerman, in southeastern Persia, are also made with the Persian knot. Warp and weft are again cotton. Kermans are worked in harmonious colors, with naturalistic flowers, chiefly roses (*Ill. 130*), though representations of animals and human beings also occur. Even portraits of historical personages are not unusual.

ISFAHAN Modern Isfahan carpets, in addition to simple *herati* or *boteh* all-over patterns, also display neoclassic designs. The Ghiordes or

Turkish knot is used; warp and weft are cotton (*Ill. 129*).

Apart from carpets made as special commissions, two types of design dominate the Persian carpet of the nineteenth century. The first is the medallion, which, although it may retain its classic form, appears also in an infinite number of variations: as a polygon with hooked or zigzag outline, linked by a pole with other medallions or medallion pendants, greatly reduced or extended as far as the border, or repeated several times along a central axis.

The second type of design is the floral motif, used as an all-over pattern. Certain standard patterns were evolved and soon found general acceptance throughout the country. Among the most popular was the *herati* (*Fig. 18*), a variation of the palmette, flanked by two leaves. Individual *herati* are linked by a network of scrolling stems, with small flower-heads in most of the empty spaces. From the distance, the impression is one of a close lattice design.

The *mina khani* pattern (*Fig. 19*) consists of large stylized rosettes of different colors arranged in straight rows and linked by scrolling stems.

The motif called in Persia a *boteh* (*Fig. 19, above*) is known in Europe under many names—pear, pine cone, almond, to mention only a few. Its closest resemblance is to a cypress swaying in the wind. Literally, *boteh* means a leaf or a bunch of leaves. *Botehs* vary in size and shape. Sometimes they are clearly outlined, sometimes made up of tiny flowers. The tip may point to the left or right, and the grouping may be close or loose. The *boteh* is also the principal feature of the Kashmir shawl. The far less common *gul hinnai* pattern, which is supposed to represent the henna plant, consists of a hyacinth-like flower surrounded by leaves.

The following pages give the names of the most important carpet groups, beginning with northwestern Persia. It must be understood in this connection that some of the most popular and commercially successful designs were taken up in many districts. Karadagh carpets, from a district on the borders of the Caucasus, closely resemble the

Caucasian Karabaghs. They are made entirely of wool, and warp and weft often include camel hair. The Ghiordes knot is used. The range of patterns is fairly wide; some favorite designs are based on bands of small flowers, *herati,* the *mina khani* pattern (*Ill.* 132), or pole medallions. The border, usually geometric or of scrolling stems, often consists of two stripes of equal width.

GOREVAN AND HEREZ   The carpets of Gorevan and Herez (*Ill.* 131) use the patterns of nearby Tabriz, but everything round becomes stylized and angular. The effect is austere, almost monumental. The Ghiordes knot is used; warp and weft are cotton. The Herez type and Karadagh carpets are sometimes called Sarabs in the trade.

FERAGHAN   Western Persia produces a great variety of carpets. Among the best-known are the Feraghans, worked on a cotton warp and weft, both in the Ghiordes and Sehna knot (*Ill.* 133). The predominating design is a *herati* all-over pattern; less often, a pole medallion on a light ground. The border consists of large palmettes and scrolling stems.

SARABEND   Sarabend carpets come from the Sarawan district. They are chiefly made with the Ghiordes knot, warp and weft being of cotton. The characteristic *boteh* (*Ill.* 134) is used as an all-over design, pointing in one row to the left and in the next to the right. The border consists of many stripes. A superior type of Sarabend carpet made at Mirabad is named Mir after its place of origin.

HAMADAN   The rugs of Hamadan, the former Ecbatana, capital of the Median kingdom, are made with the Turkish knot, on a warp and weft which may be cotton, wool, or camel hair (*Ill.* 136). Some earlier pieces have wide camel borders. The field is usually narrow and contains one or several pole medallions (*Ill.* 135). Medallion and spandrel are filled with an angular floral design, or the entire field may be covered with an all-over pattern of angular rosettes. The border includes lozenge fields, scrolling stems, animals, and occasionally a row of large *botehs.*

JOSHAGAN   Joshagan carpets are noted for the large flower-heads, scrolls, and

Fig. 19 Boteh, *or pear (above), and* mina khani *(below)*

arabesques, and borders derived from Persian carpets of the Classic
period. Warp and weft are cotton; the knot is Turkish (*Ill. 137*).

Sarouk, on the western edge of the Feraghan plain, often vied
with Kashan, and both regions employ the Classic Shah Abbas pattern. The series of concentric pendant medallions is another favorite
motif. A Classic scrolling design forms the border; the knot is
Persian, warp and weft cotton (*Ill. 138*).

SAROUK

Sultanabad, whose own carpets often show a pattern of rosettes
within lozenge-shaped fields formed by saw-edged leaves (*Ill. 141*),
was also an important center of distribution for the European trade.
Carpets used to be sent there from Muskabad and the surrounding
country. Not surprisingly—since these districts lie on the eastern
border of the Feraghan plain—there is a resemblance to Feraghan
designs. The influence of Sarouk and Kashan is also noticeable,
though Sultanabad patterns are coarser. Besides the *herati* motif
we find crow-stepped medallions; the spandrels are usually filled
with rosettes. The border, based on Classic examples, has angular
forms reminiscent of those used in Herez carpets. Sultanabads are
sometimes described as Mahals or Savalans in the trade. Warp and
weft are cotton, the knot Turkish.

SULTANABAD

45

SEHNA   Sehna (Sinneh) and Bijar rugs also belong to this group. Both provinces lie near Persia's western frontier. Though Sehna has given its name to the Persian knot, the Ghiordes or Turkish knot is often used in the carpets of this region. The designs resemble those of Feraghan and Sarabend—concentric medallions sometimes filled with *herati* and *botehs* like the rest of the field (*Ill. 139*) or an all-over pattern of *botehs* and other flowers. Again, the field may be divided into narrow horizontal bands. The border is usually narrow; warp and weft are cotton.

BIJAR   Camel hair is frequently used in the carpets of Bijar, the capital of the province of Gerrus. Though reminiscent of Sehnas in design, Bijar carpets often show Kurdish influence. Medallion and corner pieces are filled with floral motifs, the rest of the field being left bare (*Ill. 140*). Not infrequently, the pendant is shaped like a sturdy anchor. Sometimes the entire field is covered with a variety

SARAKH, LULEH   of flowers, trees, birds, and animals. These rugs are occasionally described as Sarakhs or Lulehs.

The rugs of the Kurdish nomads vary greatly. Patterns may be either traditional or adapted to a particular market. Kurdish rugs are made with the Turkish knot and are entirely of wool, in colors rather stronger than in other types of Persian rugs (*Ill. 144*). Besides the *herati* and *mina khani* patterns we find hooked medallions, perhaps the result of Caucasian influence. Many Kurdish rugs are

KURDISH, SAUJBULAGH   known in the trade as Saujbulaghs, after the chief town of Kurdistan (*Ill. 142*). Some tribes sell their rugs at Mosul, near the ancient Nineveh. Small all-over patterns, diagonal stripes, and latticework with rosettes (*Ill. 143*) are the principal field designs. Stars, hooks, and diagonal stripes form the borders. Karadja carpets are made by

MOSUL, KARADJA   the Kurds of the Hamadan region. Their principal designs are stylized plants or branches, often within latticework, or three to four lozenge-shaped medallions with hooked outline.

KERMANSHAH   Kermanshah was at one time an important center for the sale of carpets which were made both east and north of the town and therefore had considerable variety of design. The field is divided into narrow bands, or may contain a large oval or lozenge-shaped medallion with saw-edged outline, and trees and flowers of many kinds in the spandrels. The Sehna or Persian knot is used; warp and weft are cotton.

Herat, the most important town in western Afghanistan, belonged to Persia until the eighteenth century. The reputation of its carpets varies. Sometimes Herat is given as the place of origin of carpets of a splendor generally associated with the products of the Court workshops. Equally often, its importance as a carpet center is altogether doubted, and it is suggested that the town, as the former capital of Khurasan, has merely lent its name to the carpets of the province. Generally, carpets attributed to Herat have a red field with a blue or green border, or a blue field within a red border. The colors of the ground are fairly dark. The favorite motifs are large Persian flower-heads, scrolling stems, and cloud bands, and for carpets made today, *herati* or small *botehs* in rows, all facing the same direction. The Ghiordes or Turkish knot is mainly used.

The carpets of Meshed in the northeast, capital of Khurasan, have already been discussed. Other carpets made in Khurasan are noted for their size. The field often contains an all-over design, chiefly a rather complex *boteh* pattern in which small *botehs* sprout from larger ones (*Ill. 145*), or large medallions and corner pieces usually filled with floral motifs, the rest remaining bare. The field may also be divided into horizontal bands. The borders of these large carpets consist of many stripes. Warp and weft are cotton, and the knot is Persian.

Kain (Qain) carpets are also noted for their all-over designs. These include the *mina khani* pattern (*Ill. 146*), or rows of *botehs* all facing the same direction, and—above all—*herati,* since Herat, adjoining northwestern Afghanistan, is not far away. The Ghiordes knot is chiefly used; warp and weft are generally cotton.

Shiraz, the capital of Persia's southwestern province, Farsistan, is an important center of distribution, not only for its own carpets but also for the rugs of the Turkish and Arab nomads of the whole

HERAT

KHURASAN

KAIN

SHIRAZ

region. There are rugs of purely geometric designs, almost Caucasian with their angular medallions (*Ill. 147*) or closely covered field (*Ill. 148*). Again, there may be all-over *boteh* patterns of the type found in Khurasan, *botehs* of the same color forming diagonals, or a single large lozenge-shaped medallion extended as far as the border in the manner observed in the so-called Portuguese carpets. Border designs differ according to the field. This group also includes the

KASHKAI, AFSHAR

rugs of Kashkai, and of the Afshar region, farther to the east. Though the floral designs of some Afshari rugs clearly show the influence of Kerman, the principal type of decoration is geometric, with small medallions and all-over patterns. All these rugs are made entirely of wool, with the type of knot depending on the place of origin of the weaver.

ORIENTAL CARPETS IN EUROPE

More than five hundred years have passed since the first Oriental rugs came to Europe. The interest in them, both as collector's items and furnishing pieces, has in no way abated in the West during that time. There were periods when European carpets seemed more popular, but there invariably passed and the love of Persian rugs reasserted itself with even greater vigor. During the Baroque when the aim was the *Gesamtkunstwerk*, the homogenous work of art— the perfect synthesis of every part—no alien elements were allowed to intrude, and Persian carpets were of necessity out of favor.

Persian carpets of the Austrian Biedermeier period were frequently made in European designs for the Western market. The Art Nouveau at the end of the nineteenth century had little use for Oriental carpets, which would have seemed quite out of harmony with the bizarre and agitated lines of its interiors.

PERSIAN CARPETS OF THE 20TH CENTURY

In the last few decades, the export of Persian carpets has varied between 2,000 and 6,000 metric tons per year. Despite fluctuations caused by the Second World War and its aftermath, this figure surely proves that no amount of mechanical production can replace the Oriental rug. But such a heavy demand also has its adverse effects. The constant reproduction of certain designs inevitably leads to a loss of imagination and stifles the craftsman's interest in his work. Some regions of Persia have yielded to the wishes of the European and American market to such a degree that their carpets have ceased to be of any interest to the serious student.

But there is, on the other hand, hope for the future. The popular tradition survives in the tribal rugs of western and southwestern Persia. Though at times bordering on the monotonous, like all products of village industries, these rugs prove again and again that their makers are open to new impulses. Inevitably, change—to avoid the much-abused word *progress*—is slow. But very often, in many countries and in many spheres, popular art is the guardian of tradition and technique. This type of production, by being of necessity limited, is largely immune to the worst forms of commercial exploitation.

The second positive aspect in the story of the modern carpet is the revival of the Safavid tradition. Here, the aim is to make carpets to individual designs for a wealthy clientele. To this end, art schools turn out designers, factories have craftsmen available, and even the state has given every encouragement to the industry in recent years, particularly in the matter of new designs.

Obviously, designers must begin by studying the examples of the Classic age. The young artist is faced with a serious dilemma. In working out new designs, he also has to consider their appeal in the West. His task would be very much easier if his work were first to find acceptance in his own country, and then be discovered only gradually by Western carpet enthusiasts. A complete changeover from established designs would be quite disastrous in a country whose carpet exports are second only to oil in economic importance.

Consideration like these make us appreciate all the more the brilliant achievements of the Safavid dynasty. The inspired artist and the competent craftsmen need the wealthy patron. But these three find each other only rarely, and any great flowering of the arts is therefore all too brief.

INDIA

Abu-l Fazl (d. 1602), the historian of the reign of the Mogul emperor Akbar, wrote, "His majesty has caused carpets to be made of wonderful varieties and charming textures; he has appointed experienced workmen who have produced many masterpieces. The carpets of Iran [Persia] and Turan [Turkestan] are no more thought of, although merchants still import carpets from Goskhan [Joshagan], Khuzistan [southwest Persia], Kerman [southeast Persia] and Sabzwar [northeast Persia]. All kinds of carpet weavers have settled here, and drive a flourishing trade. These are found in every town, but especially in Agra, Fathpur, and Lahore." Yet surviving Indian carpets cannot be linked with any particular district.

PERSIAN INFLUENCE
FLORAL DESIGN

Carpets with an all-over design of scrolling stems, leaves, and finely drawn, giant flower-heads within a panel border undoubtedly show Persian influence (*Ill.* 87). Detailed attention to plant forms is equally characteristic both of carpets with individual flowers set within vaguely lozenge-shaped fields (*Ills.* 88, 89), and of prayer rugs, which may show single naturalistic plants in full bloom (the borders of *Ills.* 88 *and* 89) or a single shrub with hundreds of flowers of every kind (*Ill.* 86).

PRAYER RUGS

ANIMAL AND BIRD DESIGNS

The Indian love of nature, so evident in Mogul miniatures, also finds expression in animal and bird carpets (*Ill.* 91), the most famous example of which is in the Österreichische Museum für angewandte Kunst in Vienna (*Ill.* 90). All kinds of naturalistic birds, male and female, are shown in the branches and on the ground. Equal care has been lavished on the lion-mask border.

The design and workmanship of Indian carpets, always careful and detailed, make them appear typical Court products. The Indian climate hardly requires carpets, and the demand for them was therefore confined to the very wealthy. Today few carpets are made outside northern India. The leading urban centers, Srinagar, Amritsar, Lahore, Agra, Sind, and Jaipur, produce both traditional and European-influenced designs.

THE CAUCASUS

HISTORICAL CARPETS

Carpets have in all probability been made in the Caucasus for many centuries. But there is good reason why we know comparatively little about historic examples: Caucasian rugs and carpets reached Europe only via Turkey. Like many other imports, they were named after their last point of shipment in the East. Some types of fifteenth-century rugs, such as the example with the dragon and phoenixes formerly in the Berlin Museum, or the fragment with a stylized tree and two small birds in Stockholm (*Ills. 4, 5*), though generally described as Anatolian, may well have come from the Caucasus.

STRONG PERSIAN INFLUENCE

The designs of historic Caucasian carpets from the sixteenth century onward were entirely dominated by Persian influence. This fact sometimes makes attribution very difficult (*Ill. 58*).

The finest of the early Persian vase carpets (*Ill. 55*) display a profusion of flowering plants, imaginary flowers, and vases on a ground of uniform color. The composition is governed by three separate systems of scrolling stems, within a border of delicate scrolls and giant flower-heads seen from above (rosettes). A large, obviously related group of early Caucasian carpets (*Ill. 59*), also with the field of a uniform color, contains either two systems of scrolling stems, or one system of scrolling stems which enclose small lozenge-shaped

VERY NARROW BORDER

fields (*Ill. 73*). All these carpets have extremely narrow borders, with large stylized flowers or small blossoms in square arrangements.

Such an unbalanced relationship between field and border is unthinkable in a Persian carpet of the Safavid period. It would probably be quite safe to describe this group as Caucasian. Besides carpets in which every detail (vases, giant flower-heads, plants) is extremely finely drawn, we find pieces with almost angular floral designs. The center of many of these large flower-heads often resembles a berry. This form, enlarged and with a lozenge pattern, recurs in the so-called dragon carpets (*Ills. 73, 75 to 77*). We look in vain for dragons. Originally, the design represented animals individually or in combat, a subject well known from Persian sixteenth-century carpets. In Caucasian rugs, these animals are distorted horizontally beyond recognition. Plant and animal forms become increasingly stylized (*Ills. 74, 80, 84*) and block-like. Outlines are flared, stepped, or hooked.

ABSENCE OF DRAGONS

In all-over patterns, the preference is for large flower-heads and arabesques with almost angular, forked ends. Scrolling often appears as a taut line, stretched from flower to flower (*Ills. 78, 81*). Such extreme stylization is a chief characteristic of old Caucasian rugs, but increasing coarsening and stylization of Persian motifs continued for generations. The proportion of field to border, so carefully observed in Persian carpets, counted for very little with Caucasian weavers. Quite the contrary: when the huge field design seems to swamp everything, the border is still usually very narrow, almost meager.

PROPORTION OF FIELD TO BORDER

But though the Caucasus had many rulers—Turkoman, Turkish, Persian, and Russian—and is separated into north and south by tall mountain ranges, the carpets of the entire region have much in common. The Ghiordes or Turkish knot is used throughout; warp and weft are mostly wool, hardly ever cotton. Floral motifs, if used at all, are highly stylized. Preference is for vigorous geometric forms, polygons, stars, and lozenges derived from the Persian medallion (*Figs. 20 to 25*). The geographic position alone would make the adoption of new designs unlikely. Vegetables dyes have never been

COMMON CHARACTERISTICS

Fig. 20 Caucasian border, ca. *1600*

abandoned, and the characteristic carpet colors, red, blue, brown, yellow, green, and ivory, retain their importance.

DAGHESTAN

Daghestan—"mountain land"—lies in the northeast of the Caucasus on the shores of the Caspian Sea. Its capital was Derbent—"the gate"; a little farther south is the town of Kuba. Daghestans are patterned with a variety of small motifs, diagonally arranged and changing in color (*Ill. 149*): *botehs,* carnations, and trefoils, as well as medallions, stars, and stylized rosettes. Borders may contain S-forms, angular designs, or hook motifs. The mihrab always has an angular outline and is filled with stylized flowers (*Fig. 150*).

DERBENT

Derbent rugs may also display the *boteh* or a lattice design with stylized flowers. Sometimes there is a diagonal arrangement of larger rosettes. A very characteristic feature is arabesques with split ends; stars or hooked lozenges also occur (*Ill. 151*).

KUBA, KABISTAN

Other members of the same group are the rugs of Kuba (*Ill. 153*), with medallions containing large radiating stars or octagons, and Kabistan (*Ill. 154*), with rosettes, arabesques, occasionally *botehs,* and vaguely Kufic borders.

LEZGHIAN

Lezghians, from west of Daghestan, are a type of nomad rug with designs based on hooked lozenges, octagons, stars, S-forms, and

Fig. 21 Caucasian palmette, seventeenth century

geometric borders (*Ill. 152*). Chichi rugs are made by the Chu- CHICHI CARPETS
chenses tribe, north of the Lezghian locale. The principal motifs
are S-forms, *botehs,* and rosettes, arranged horizontally. The border
of rosettes and diagonal bands is almost European in character
(*Ill. 156*).

In Seichur rugs, the space between the characteristic medallions SEICHUR
with their lozenge-shaped bands is filled with small flowers (*Ill.
157*).

The Circassians, on the banks of the Black Sea, almost invariably CIRCASSIAN
use flared medallions.

Shirvan, with the towns of Baku and Shemakha, is south of SHIRVAN
Daghestan. Shirvan rugs display a variety of designs. Lozenge fields
outlined with hooks and occupying almost the entire width are not
uncommon, nor are octagons, cruciform medallions, or medallions

Fig. 22   Reciprocal trefoil border, seventeenth-century Polonaise rug

narrowing horizontally (*Ill. 155*), as well as hexagonal latticework, diagonal stripes, S-forms, and small animals.

BAKU   The colors of Baku rugs, somewhat duller, are chiefly browns, blues, yellows, and black (*Ill. 158*). Favorite motifs are small cruciform medallions and angular *botehs* surrounded by small flowers, though the design is never limited to these. Borders of between three and five stripes include scrolling stems and carnations.

SHEMAKHA   Certain rugs made in Shemakha, the capital of Shirvan, are occasionally called "Royal Daghestan" in the trade. Designs mostly consist of stylized flowers and lozenge-shaped fields (*Ill. 160*). A more important product of the town are the so-called Soumaks, rugs and carpets woven in a technique described in another chapter (*Ill. 159*). Designs consist of three or four horizontally elongated medallions, with a symmetric arrangement of octagons covering the rest of the field.

Fig. 23   Caucasian arabesque

KAZAK

Kazak rugs, made by the women of the Kazak tribe, are proof that geometric designs can be far from monotonous. Medallions of every kind (*Ills. 161, 162*), hook forms, and every conceivable type of polygon appear. Occasionally, the name is extended to rugs without any coherent pattern.

KARABAGH

Karabagh Province, southwest of Shirvan, is on the river Aras near the Persian border. Its rugs have geometric designs, mainly lozenge-shaped fields formed by saw-edged bands or broad leaves, and filled with stylized flowers (*Ill. 163*). The field may also be completely bare. The rugs of Shusha, the capital, contain medallions and corner pieces with stylized flowers (*Ill. 164*), with a few stylized flowers in the rest of the field. They appear altogether more Persian in character.

GENDJEH

Gendjeh (Ghenga) rugs used to be sold in the market of Elisavetpol, known as Gandzha under Persian rule and today called Kirovabad. They are nomad rugs, with much white, and resemble Kazaks

57

in the variety and choice of motifs. We find diagonal stripes, hooked lozenges, crosses, rectangles, and wide reciprocal zigzag borders. The number of knots per square inch is few, there being several rows of weaving after each row of knots (*Ill. 165*).

KUTAIS   Kutais, once capital of Imeritia, a highly fertile region, lies farther west. Its rugs resemble the Kazaks. Frequently, the narrow field is divided into horizontal stripes and surrounded by a wide multiple border. When *botehs* occur, they have long angular tips.

TALISH, GHILAN   The rugs of Talish and Ghilan (Gilan), on the southwestern shores of the Caspian Sea, are already Persian, although in character their designs—the Talish with a bare field and geometric rosette border, the Ghilan with *botehs,* stepped medallions and corner pieces—are Caucasian rather than Persian.

VERNEH   Two types of Caucasian woven carpets or rugs must not be forgotten. Verneh, near Shusha, has produced rugs with stylized animals and birds within square fields (*Ill. 166*), or animals and small SILEH   ornamental devices arranged in diagonal stripes. The rugs of Sileh are noted for their large animals, stylized into Z- or S-forms and recognizable only from the tiny feet (*Ill. 167*).

Figs. 24 and 25   Typical Caucasian borders.

TURKESTAN

Like the Caucasus, Turkestan has seen a succession of conquerors, from Medes, Persians, Tatars, Mongols, Greeks, and Romans, to Turks, Russians, and Chinese.

Shades of red, from a very rich color to almost purple, predominate in Turkoman and related rugs from Western Turkestan and the surrounding regions. Other colors, such as dark blue and ivory play only a subordinate part. Knotting—almost invariably the Sehna or Persian knot—is very close, the pile usually short. Goat's hair as well as sheep's wool is used. RED TO ALMOST PURPLE

The province of Bokhara (Bukhara), now Uzbekistan and part of Russia, extended from the Oxus to the Pamir plateau. Its chief city, also named Bokhara, was the intellectual center of Asia. Caravans from China, India, Persia, and Russia passed through it, and carpets made by the tribes of the whole region were sold there, whence the caravans took them to Russia to be sold again in the markets of Astrakhan, Orenburg, and Nizhni Novgorod. The finest examples, chiefly Tekkes, were known in the trade as "Royal Bokhara," or just Bokhara. BOKHARA

ROYAL BOKHARA

The name Bokhara is still widely used, particularly in England, but it is misleading. It is better to call the rugs and carpets of this group by the names of the tribes who make them. The chief characteristic of the entire group is the so-called *gul,* a kind of emblem, which varies with each tribe. It may be square, polygonal, star-shaped, etc. These medallions are usually quartered, opposite quarters having the same color (red or white). A very common feature is the wide end borders, generally woven and patterned. TYPICAL MARKS, GULS

59

KHATCHLI, PRINCESS
BOKHARA

Smaller rugs used as tent flaps are known as Khatchlis or Hachlis, after the cruciform design which divides the field into four. They are still frequently described as "Princess Bokharas." Examples with one or several mihrabs were probably intended as prayer rugs. Knotted tent bags, the larger called Jowals and the smaller Torbas, were also made.

JOWALS, TORBAS

TEKKES

In the rugs and carpets of the Tekke tribe, the characteristic *guls,* usually three or four rows, are placed at the intersecting points of a network of thin lines (*Ill. 168*). The space between is filled with a system of smaller star-shaped medallions; end-borders are formed by a zigzag design.

SALORS

The Salor-Turkomans prefer wide octagonal *guls* with hooked and zigzag outlines, interspersed with small elongated polygons (*Ill. 169*).

The Pendeh-Turkomans use quartered polygons, with a system of similar smaller polygons between (*Ill. 170*), but without a line network. Pendeh Khatchlis have five or even more small mihrabs with a treelike form below, and a scatter design remotely resembling scrolling stems in the rest of the field.

PENDEHS

KHIVAS

The Khiva-Turkomans live in an area between the left bank of the Amu Darya River and the Aral Sea. Some of their rugs, with leaves, scrolling stems, animals, and geometric designs, show Caucasian influence. A favorite motif is lozenges outlined in dark blue. In Khatchlis, these are often arranged on vertical lines (*Ill. 171*). Another name for Khivas is Kisilayaks.

KISILAYAKS

YOMUDS

The Yomud tribe produces rugs with widely spaced small polygons arranged in alternating rows (*Ill. 177*), though hooked lozenges alternating with almost circular small medallions also appear. The borders are formed by zigzag motifs with hooked outlines. In Yomud Khatchlis the areas between the arms of the cross are covered with closely spaced, highly stylized flowers within a stylized rosette border and zigzag end borders (*Ill. 178*).

BESHIR

Beshir rugs and carpets, from the region near the Afghan border, display a wider range of motifs than other members of this group. We frequently find cloud bands and dots (*Ill. 174*), or a lattice design dividing the field into lozenges or similar forms, which in turn are filled with smaller lozenges and octagons (*Ill. 172*). The field may also be split up into bands enclosing scrolling stems, nor are cruciform medallions with stepped outline unusual. Beshirs resembling Yomuds were often called "Blue Bokharas," though the terms is hardly ever used now. In Beshir prayer rugs, the field of the somewhat flat-gabled mihrab, usually divided into a white outer and a red inner section, contains several systems of flowering stems, some straight and some scrolling. In general, red predominates less in Beshirs than in other Turkoman rugs, and in addition to the characteristic reddish brown, a deep, dark blue often is used. The drawing is yellow and white.

BLUE BOKHARA

The so-called Afghans, from the region between Bokhara and Hindu Kush, have nothing in common with the carpets of Herat (the leading city in western Afghanistan, long under Persian rule), which are discussed in the chapter on Persia. Afghan *guls,* usually octagonal and closely spaced in three rows, are quarted in a lighter red and dark blue. They contain smaller lozenges and quatrefoil leaves, and are linked by a system of smaller polygons and stiff stems. An angular scroll forms the border. Occasionally the Ghiordes knot is used instead of the Sehna.

AFGHAN

HERAT

The manufacture of *Baluchi* carpets and rugs, the coarsest in this group, extends as far as southeast Persia. The range of motifs is wide, including large octagons, hooked lozenges both large and small and sometimes forming diagonal bands, and a floral design resembling the *mina khani* pattern. In prayer rugs, the mihrab has a square gable and contains a tree with large, saw-edged leaves.

BALUCHI

The carpets of Eastern Turkestan, entirely different in character, show strong Chinese influence. Many of the characteristic Chinese motifs appear, both in the field and in the border. Blue, yellow, and ivory, as well as shades of red, govern the color schemes. Round

EAST-TURKESTAN AND

CHINESE INFLUENCE

medallions (*Ill. 182*), square fields enclosing Chinese symbols (*Ill. 179*), lattice designs, and stiff flowering stems are found again and again in these carpets, products of Kashgar (*Ill. 180*), Yarkend, Khotan (*Ill. 182*), and Samarkand (*Ills. 179 and 181*), the last a name often used for the whole group because of its being the principal center of distribution in the East. The same family includes silk rugs and family prayer rugs called Saphs, in which the several mihrabs, often of different colors, may be either plain or filled with floral designs (*Ill. 181*).

CHINA

Knotted carpets did not appear in China until fairly late and are therefore of comparatively little historical importance. Apart from early finds in Eastern (Chinese) Turkestan, which have apparently remained isolated, there is hardly a Chinese carpet that can be attributed to a date earlier than the seventeenth century.

THE 17TH CENTURY

But China has made a unique contribution, the pillar rug. It is not intended to lie flat on the floor, but to go around a pillar (*Ill. 94*), as is evident from the design, usually standing figures or dragons, which appear complete only when the sides of the carpet are joined. The lower end border is formed by symbols of rocks and waves, the upper by a variety of motifs. Although the carpets of Kashgar, Khotan, and Yarkend all contain some Persian, Turkoman, and Chinese elements, Chinese craftsmen keep strictly to an ancient native tradition. Besides continuous floral scrolls we find fan, sword, magic gourd and iron staff, bamboo clappers, basket of flowers, drum, flute, and lotus flowers, the Taoist emblems of the Eight Immortals; also the eight symbols of Buddhism: wheel, conch shell, umbrella, canopy, vase, two fishes, and knot; or the Hundred Treasures, such as pearls, money, stone gong, drinking horn, artemisia leaf, etc. Favorite animals include dragons, phoenixes, bats, and Fu dogs; favorite flowers, the lotus, chrysanthemum, and peony. There are also cloud bands, symbols for mountains, rocks, fire, and

PILLAR RUG

MOTIFS

RELIEF EFFECT

water, and purely geometric forms like the Chinese key-fret or meander (*Ills. 92, 93, Fig. 26*). The knot count is lower than in most Oriental carpets, the pile long. The relief-like effect of more recent Chinese carpets is achieved by clipping the pile around the design. Warp and weft are cotton; the pile is generally wool, occasionally silk. Chief centers of production—as in the past—are the four northern provinces, Kansu, Shansi, Shensi, and Chihli.

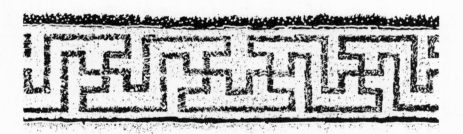

Fig. 26   Chinese meander or key-fret pattern

*Fig. 27   Section of a map published in 1700, giving many of the
principal regions of carpet manufacture*

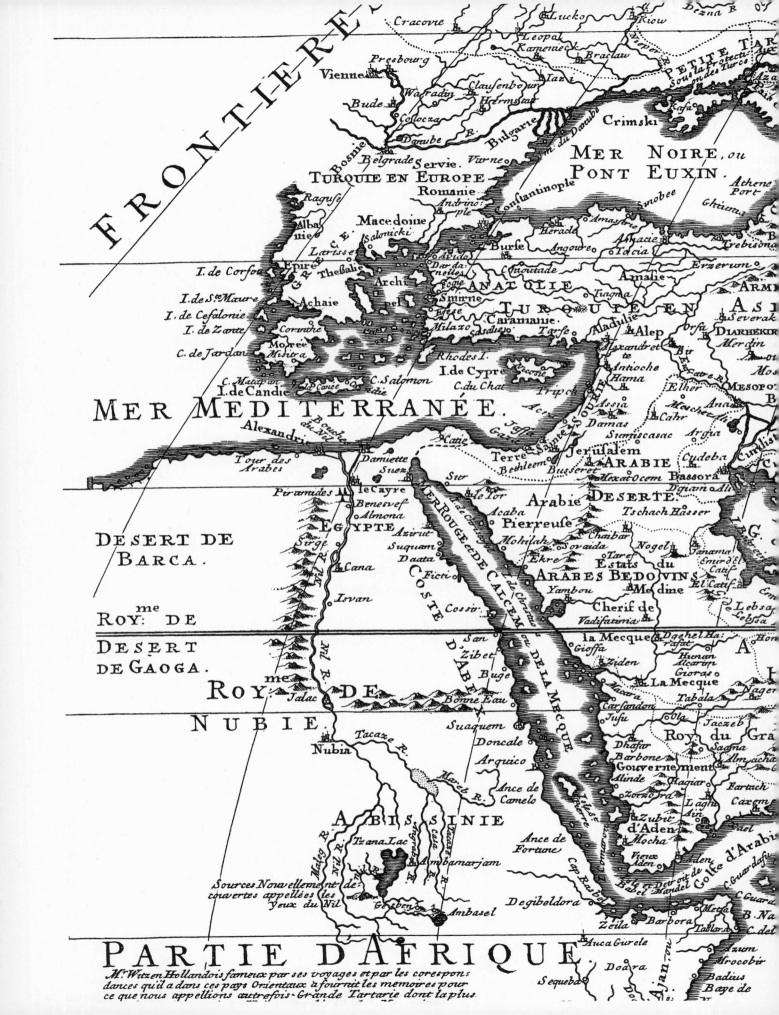

PARTIE D'AFRIQUE

Mr. Witzen Hollandois fameux par ses voyages et par les corespon:
dances qu'il a dans ces pays Orientaux a fournit les memoires pour
ce que nous appellions autrefois Grande Tartarie dont la plus.

EUROPEAN CARPETS

SPAIN

Spain, through the Moorish occupation closely connected with the Islamic world, has served as a gateway to Europe where the arts and crafts of the Middle East are concerned. The technique of tin glaze (Majolica) reached Italy via Spain, and Spain was also the first European country to import, and later produce, knotted car- FIRST EUROPEAN KNOTTED CARPETS pets in quantity. In the second half of the thirteenth century, Queen Eleanor of Castile brought the first carpets to England, where they aroused much admiration as well as criticism.

Though the earliest surviving Spanish examples belong to the fifteenth century, they closely resemble the medieval Seljuk carpets SELJUK in character. The field is usually covered with an all-over design, to which the Spanish weaver has added a few coats-of-arms. Kufic characters appear in the border, though they have lost their vigor and become rather delicate. Tiny plaitwork and elaborately inter- laced arabesques are everywhere.

That the geometric decor—squares, polygons, stylized flowers and rosettes—of Anatolian carpets should have been adopted in sixteenth- century Europe is hardly surprising in view of the extensive imports from the Middle East (*Ills. 99, 100*). Almost simultaneously, Spanish carpet designs passed through another stage. Contemporary velvet and brocade designs, strongly influenced by the demands of CHURCH AND COURT INFLUENCE Church and Court, began to appear. Animals back-to-back, eagles both one- and two-headed, lions, griffins, coats-of-arms, the "pome-granate" pattern, fields divided by interlacing ropes, borders filled with the scrolls and grotesques of the Renaissance, and the lavish use of Christian and heraldic emblems are among the chief characteristics of Spanish carpets from the late fifteenth to the seventeenth century (*Ills. 101 to 104*). Compared to typically Spanish products, other carpets made more or less in adaptation of Turkish (Ushak) and Persian examples are of small historic significance.

ALMERÍA, CUENCA, ALCARAZ

In the early Middle Ages, Spanish carpets were chiefly made in Almería, from the eleventh century onward in Cuenca, and later—until the seventeenth century—in Alcaraz.

SPANISH TECHNIQUE

The Spanish technique differs completely from that of the East. A single warp knot is used, the knots being tied only on every other warp thread, but alternating in each row.

ALPUJARRA

In the eighteenth century, the Spanish carpet was reduced to the level of popular art. No longer knotted, it became a looped woven fabric or an embroidery. Practically all these rugs are known as Alpujarras, after the mountainous Alpujarra region, south of the Sierra Nevada, where they were made.

In the medallion, pendants, and corner pieces we find genii; in the rest of the field, animals in pursuit and in combat. The landscape is indicated by flowering trees. The main border stripe consists of panels with animals and small flowers; identical flowering scrolls appear in the guard stripes.

214 x 146 cm. (7 ft. x 4 ft. 9 in.) Österreichisches Museum für angewandte Kunst, Vienna. Bequest of Clarice de Rothschild.

PLATE VIII   KNOTTED WOOLEN CARPET; CHINESE,
18TH/19TH CENTURY

On the dark blue ground, as the central motif, is a yellow tree peony
with red flowers. Meander and peony border stripes.
335 x 240 cm. (11 ft. x 8 ft. 2 in.) Österreichisches Museum für angewandte
Kunst, Vienna. Bequest of Anton Exner.

ENGLAND

In the early sixteenth century, the account books of noble English households still listed sums spent on "rushes, bents, bracken." Obviously the carpets introduced in earlier centuries had had few successors. Yet it is highly probable that the returning Crusaders brought rugs home with them long before the arrival of the dowry of Queen Eleanor of Castile in 1255.

In 1520, the Signoria of Venice presented Cardinal Wolsey with 16TH CENTURY a handsome gift of carpets through its ambassador Sebastiano Giustiniani. The number is uncertain. Sometimes there is mention of sixty, then of a hundred pieces, usually described as "Damascene DAMASCENE CARPETS carpets." There is increasing reference in contemporary records to "tapis of Turque" and "carpytts of Turque makynge." ANATOLIAN INFLUENCES

An English carpet with the arms and motto of Queen Elizabeth I and an all-over pattern of flowering branches and carnations bears the date 1570. Several surviving examples from the eighties of the same century are free copies of Ushak designs; others, slightly later, of geometric Anatolian rugs. Dates, coats-of-arms, and a technical HEMP OR FLAX detail—cotton or flax were used in England for warp and weft— seem a clear indication of the common origin of these carpets (*Ill. 105*).

Interest grew to such an extent that, according to Hakluyt's *Voyages,* "M. Morgan Hubblethorn, Dier," was sent to Persia in

1579 to study and, if possible, to "procure a singular good workman in the art of Turkish carpet making."

With the advancing seventeenth century, Oriental motifs yielded to naturalistic flowers, the typical textile design of the age, well known from brocades and embroideries. Soon the ground was covered so thickly by a profusion of bright flowers that the connecting scrolling stems or tendrils completely disappeared. In character, these carpets are not unlike the floral inlays of contemporary English furniture (*Ill. 106*).

We know little of English carpets during the next few decades. There was a revival in the middle of the eighteenth century, when a Frenchman, Pierre Parisot, set himself up in Paddington with two carpet-weavers who had formerly worked at the Chaillot factory near Paris. Parisot found a wealthy patron in the Duke of Cumberland, and two years later, in 1752, the first carpet from his workshop was presented to the widow of the Prince of Wales. Quarrels with the two French weavers led to their dismissal and their replacement by English workmen. The factory moved to Fulham, closed down in 1755.

The Royal Society of Arts, anxious to preserve the craft of making carpets, offered several rewards. Among the winners were Thomas Whitty, Passavant, and Thomas Moore.

Whitty was the founder of the Axminster factory, which lasted until 1835, when it was transferred to Wilton, near Salisbury.

Passavant had taken over Parisot's Fulham factory, which he moved to Exeter to be closer to the center of the wool trade.

Moore, whose workshops were at Moorfields in the City, carried out a series of large commissions, including carpets to designs by Robert Adam.

English eighteenth- and early nineteenth-century designs are entirely dominated by the influence of the French Savonnerie factory and the demands of Rococo and Classic Revival architects. The carpet frequently had to mirror the stucco design of the ceiling.

In later years, England could claim all the decisive contributions to machine production, from the use of colored chenille strips to mechanical knotting.

FRANCE

Two names, Aubusson and Savonnerie, at once come to mind with any mention of French carpets. Aubusson, in the Creuse region near Limoges, another leading center of the crafts, has produced tapestries, carpets, and bedspreads, as well as wall hangings, for many centuries (*Ill. 111*). Its reputation was so secure that later factories in Beauvais, Fontainebleau, and Paris could not replace it, and the name Aubusson remained, especially for knotted floor-covering, no matter where it was actually manufactured. Even today Aubusson carpets are very much in demand because of their quality and beauty.

The names of Jean Fortier and Pierre Dupont are of particular importance in the history of French carpets. In 1601, Fortier claimed to be able to make carpets in the Oriental manner. Three years later, Dupont made the same assertion in *La Stromatourgie,* a treatise dedicated to Henri IV. Dupont was given a workshop in the Louvre, but brisk trade made it necessary to transfer at least part of the business to more spacious quarters. Dupont himself stayed in the Louvre; his pupil Simon Lourdet moved to the "Hospice de la Savonnerie" at Chaillot, then a small suburb of Paris. The Hospice, formerly a soap factory, had become a children's home. For Lourdet, the move meant a steady supply of labor; for the Hospice—after which the carpets were named—financial help. Each of the children was put

AUBUSSON

JEAN FORTIER, PIERRE DUPONT

SIMON LOURDET

75

to work in the factory for twelve years, the Hospice receiving an annual sum.

Louis XIII protected French factories by a ban on Oriental and other carpets; only French carpets could be offered for sale in

SAVONNERIE France. By 1672, the entire carpet works was concentrated at Savonnerie, under the control of Dupont's son and Lourdet's widow.

CARPETS FOR THE COURT Commissions from the Court were always considerable. For instance, Louis XIV ordered no less than ninety carpets for the Grande Galerie in the Louvre. These were delivered in 1685. The increasing general prosperity and great building activity were bound to affect the carpet industry, and the demand grew rapidly; soon carpets were a favorite gift to foreign rulers.

In 1825, the Savonnerie factory, which survived the Revolution and Napoleon, became part of the Manufacture Nationale des Gobelins, the official state factory.

A close pattern of gaily colored flowers predominates in early examples of French carpets. During the reign of Louis XIV the influence of architects grew steadily, and in consequence Savon-

CHANGE OF TASTE neries faithfully reflect the changes of taste from Baroque to Classicism, and again the "Second Rococo" (*Ills. 107 to 110*). Warp and weft are generally flax; the knot is Turkish. To accelerate knotting, the pattern-forming thread is wound across a thin iron rod that terminates in a blade. As the rod is pulled out, the loops are cut open. This process is also employed in the making of velvet (*Fig. 28*).

KNOTTING - PROCESS The large designs used in French carpets permit a comparatively small number of knots per square inch, despite a wide and finely graduated range of color.

Tapis de Turquie, l'enlacement des fils pour faire le Naud et manière de tirer le Tranche fil pour couper les points et former le Télouté

Fig. 28 Knotting

Fig. 29   At the loom

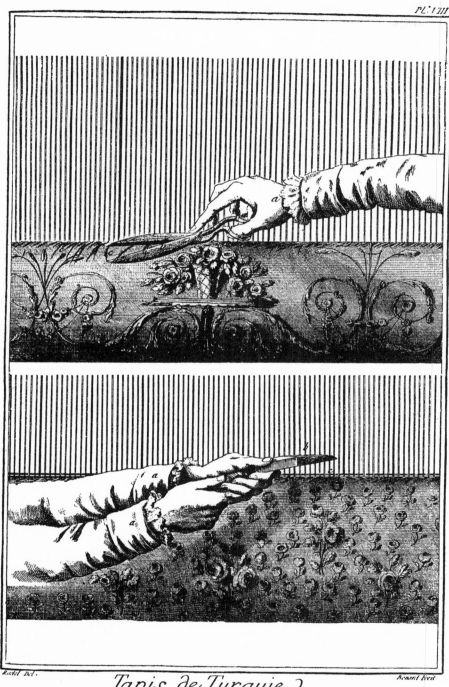

Pl. VIII

Tapis de Turquie,
Service des Ciseaux courbes, et Service du Peigne

Fig. 30 (above): Trimming a row
          (below): Beating down

79

GALLERY OF RUGS

1

I. KNOTTED WOOLEN RUG FROM PAZYRYK; 5TH CENTURY B.C.

The central field is covered with a quatrefoil pattern. The border, of five parts, shows horsemen and deer in the wider stripes, griffins within small squares and rosettes in the guard stripes. The colors are red, light blue, a greenish-yellow, and orange; the horsemen are light against a red background, the deer red against a light background. The earliest known knotted carpet.

200 x 183 cm. (6 ft. 7 in. x 6 ft.) Ghiordes or Turkish knot, 225 knots per sq. in. Hermitage Museum, Leningrad.

ANATOLIA (Asia Minor)

Early Anatolian carpets usually display geometric patterns or highly stylized plants and animals. Geometric designs predominate increasingly (for some time also in Persian carpets) until the sixteenth century, when this trend is reversed and even Anatolian carpets begin to show Persian influence.

2. KNOTTED WOOLEN CARPET FROM THE MOSQUE OF ALA-AD-DIN, KONYA; CENTRAL ANATOLIAN, 13TH CENTURY

The field is covered with a stylized plant pattern, dark red on light red. The calligraphic or Kufic border (here grayish-blue on black), is an important feature of many Anatolian carpets.

520 x 285 cm. (17 ft. x 9 ft. 4 in.) Türk ve Islam Eserleri Müzesi, Istanbul.

3. KNOTTED WOOLEN CARPET FROM THE MOSQUE OF ALA-AD-DIN, KONYA; CENTRAL ANATOLIAN, 13TH CENTURY

In the black field a pattern of red octagonal stars is linked by stylized Kufic characters. The principal border contains a geometric design in light red on a darker ground; in the guard stripes are smaller squares with pairs of volutes. This pattern appears in many Turkish carpets made between the fifteenth and seventeenth centuries.

320 x 240 cm. (10 ft. 6 in. x 7 ft. 10 in.) Türk ve Islam Eserleri Müzesi, Istanbul.

2

3

4. KNOTTED WOOLEN RUG; ANATOLIAN, EARLY 15TH CENTURY

There are two octagons within rectangles, the sides decorated with latch hooks on a yellow field. Within each rectangle a stylized tree is flanked by birds with crests of two feathers and tails of three. In the three border stripes are rectangles bisected diagonally, and small angular scrolls. From the Parish Church at Marby (Jämtland), Sweden.

145 x 109 cm. (4 ft. 10 in. x 3 ft. 7 in.) Ghiordes or Turkish knot, 47 knots per sq. in. Statens Historiska Museet, Stockholm.

5. KNOTTED WOOLEN RUG; ANATOLIAN, EARLY 15TH CENTURY

The two rectangles contain octagons with dragons and phoenixes (blue, outlined in red) on a yellow ground; the border, S-forms and small lozenges. Carpets of a similar design appear in Italian paintings of the Early Renaissance. From a church in central Italy.

172 x 90 cm. (5 ft. 8 in. x 2 ft. 11 in.) Ghiordes or Turkish knot, 50 knots per sq. in. Formerly in Islamic section, Staatliche Museen, Berlin.

4

5

6

6. FRAGMENT OF A KNOTTED WOOLEN RUG; WESTERN ANATOLIA, END OF THE 15TH CENTURY

The two main decorative elements, octagons and a cruciform motif, are arranged in alternate rows. Small rosettes fill the gaps. The border design is based on two Kufic characters, which alternate throughout.
159 x 137 cm. (5 ft. 3 in. x 4 ft. 6 in.) Formerly in Islamic section, Staatliche Museen, Berlin. Now missing.

7. KNOTTED WOOLEN RUG; WESTERN ANATOLIA, 16TH CENTURY

The octagons are enclosed in a network of loosely formed medallions. The design of the border is based on Kufic characters. Rugs of this kind inspired the earliest Spanish carpets.
242 x 137 cm. (7 ft. 11 in. x 4 ft. 6 in.) Formerly in Islamic section, Staatliche Museen, Berlin. Now missing.

8. KNOTTED WOOLEN RUG; WESTERN ANATOLIA, 17TH CENTURY

The field contains polygons formed by interlacement bands; the border, severely stylized scrolls. A later, simpler interpretation of the pattern is shown in *Ill. 6*.
158 x 114 cm. (5 ft. 2 in. x 3 ft. 9 in.) Formerly in Islamic section, Staatliche Museen, Berlin.

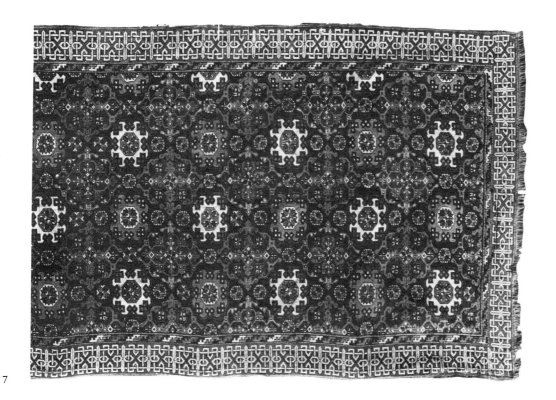

7

8

9. KNOTTED WOOLEN CARPET; WESTERN ANATOLIA, 16TH CENTURY

In the field are octagons within rectangles, framed by rows of smaller octagons. The two central octagons are filled with converging leaves. The triple border is formed by a calligraphic frieze, rosettes, and angular scrolls. This type of decoration returns in the Bergama rugs of later centuries.

427 x 190 cm. (14 ft. x 6 ft. 3 in.) Formerly in Islamic section, Staatliche Museen, Berlin.

10

10. KNOTTED WOOLEN CARPET; USHAK, CA. 1600

In the center of the field is an almost circular medallion filled with scrolls and arabesques; at the corner are lobed half-medallions. Blue scrolling stems wind across the red field. The principal border stripe contains flowering branches; the guard stripes, angular scrolls. Red and dark blue are the dominant colors. The Persian medallion pattern has found acceptance in Asia Minor.

425 x 136 cm. (13 ft. 11 in. x 4 ft. 5 in.)Österreichisches Museum für angewandte Kunst, Vienna.

11. KNOTTED WOOLEN CARPET; STAR-USHAK, FIRST HALF 17TH CENTURY

Large octagonal stars alternate with lozenge-shaped stars. Within the stars are arabesques; on the red ground are flowering branches. The three border stripes are formed by angular scrolls. The decoration of Star-Ushaks is somewhat more geometric than that of the slightly earlier Medallion Ushaks (*Ill. 10*).
305 x 185 cm. (10 ft. x 6 ft. 1 in.) Kölnisches Stadtmuseum, Zeughaus, Cologne.

13

12. KNOTTED WOOLEN RUG; WESTERN ANATOLIA (USHAK REGION), 17TH CENTURY

A network of yellow arabesque and angular scrolls stands out against the red ground. In the upper right-hand corner appear the arms of the Centurione and Doria families of Genoa. A scrolling stem with almond-shaped leaves and rosettes decorates the principal border stripe; more scrolling stems can be seen in the guard stripes. This type of rug is still known as a Holbein carpet, though it does not appear in any picture by the younger Holbein. The pattern is used not only in the rugs of Asia Minor and the Caucasus, but also in English carpets. Persian influence has now almost completely yielded to severely geometric stylization.

209 x 141 cm. (6 ft. 10 in. x 4 ft. 7 in.) Museum für Kunst und Gewerbe, Hamburg.

13. KNOTTED WOOLEN CARPET; WESTERN ANATOLIA (USHAK REGION), CA. 1700

On the dark field are two large diamonds within light and agitated outlines. Within each is an octagon with a stylized flower; in the gaps between, flowering scrolls. In the border stripe are stylized lilies within rectangles; the guard stripes consist of S-forms. A coarser and simplified version of the Star-Ushak.

250 x 160 cm. (8 ft. 2 in. x 5 ft. 3 in.) Formerly in the Pohlmann Collection, Berlin.

14

CARPETS OF TURKISH COURT MANUFACTURE

The products of Turkish Court manufacture, whatever their place of origin, are entirely Persian in character, probably because they were made by Persian craftsmen working to Persian designs.

14. WOOLEN PRAYER RUG; TURKISH COURT MANUFACTURE, 16TH CENTURY

A tripartite mihrab, the middle field green, the others red. The three arches are supported by pillars; between these, at the lower edge, are flowers. A lamp hangs down from the center arch. In the cross panel are trees and pavilions; in the light blue border, *herati,* giant flower-heads, lanceolate leaves, carnations, and hyacinths; the guard stripes contain rosettes. This prayer rug can be considered the forerunner of the Pillar Ladik.

Courtesy of the Metropolitan Museum of Art, New York. Gift of James F. Ballard, 1922.

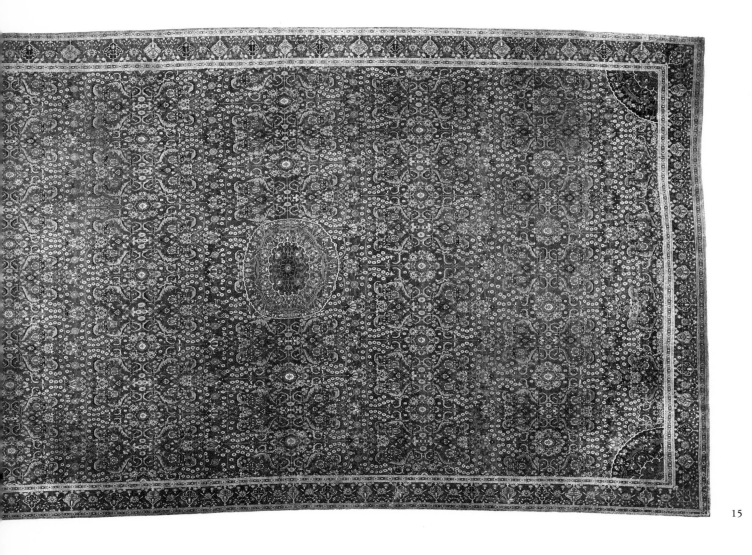

15. KNOTTED WOOLEN CARPET; TURKISH COURT MANUFACTURE, 16TH CENTURY

The red ground is filled with a pattern of rosettes, leaves, and flowering branches. Medallion and corner pieces are small and circular, with flowers and cloud bands. In contrast to Persian examples, the medallion is almost swamped by the all-over decoration.

728 x 419 cm. (23 ft. 10 in. x 13 ft. 9 in.) On silk, Sehna or Persian knot, 200 knots per sq. in. Österreichisches Museum für angewandte Kunst, Vienna.

16

16. KNOTTED WOOLEN RUG; TURKISH COURT MANUFACTURE, 16TH CENTURY

On the red ground a light blue medallion encloses an arabesque, flowering branches, and lilies; the corner pieces are filled with arabesques. The rest of the field is covered with a pattern of dots and cloud bands. A particularly fine feature, as in most rugs of this type, is the wide border—here of giant flower-heads and flowering scrolls—with its identical guard stripes.

190 x 132 cm. (6 ft. 3 in. x 4 ft. 4 in.) Sehna or Persian knot, approx. 140 knots per sq. in. Formerly Islamic section, Staatliche Museen, Berlin.

17. KNOTTED WOOLEN RUG; TURKISH COURT MANUFACTURE, 16TH CENTURY

A small round medallion is centered in the field, surrounded by large flower-heads merging into a pattern of flowering scrolls; between these is a garland with large rosettes. In the principal border stripe are two intersecting systems of flowering scrolls; in the guard stripes, rosettes. The influence of this design is very noticeable in the Damascus ("Ottoman") carpets of Cairo (*Ill.* 97).

198 x 136 cm. (6 ft. 6 in. x 4 ft. 5 in.) Department for crafts and sculpture, Städtisches Kunstmuseum, Düsseldorf.

18. KNOTTED WOOLEN RUG; TURKISH COURT MANUFACTURE, 16TH CENTURY

At the center of the field a small round medallion is filled with tulips and carnations; at the corners are similar quarter medallions. Elsewhere the design, oriented toward the middle, consists of lanceolate leaves, imaginary flowers, hyacinths, and—on the right and left—an arrangement of feathery leaves and large flowers. The principal border stripe contains imaginary flowers, tulips, carnations and hyacinths; the tripartite guard stripes are identical. Here, too, the medallion is almost swamped by the rich pattern.

221 x 157 cm. (7 ft. 3 in. x 5 ft. 1 in.) Musée des arts decoratifs, Paris.

18

19. KNOTTED WOOLEN CARPET; TURKISH COURT MANUFACTURE, CA. 1600

Repeated four times in the field is a design based on a rosette surrounded by four flowers and dense leaves, further embellished with palmettes, flowering branches, and more foliage. In the border, white-framed round and oblong fields are filled with flowers; the two guard stripes are identical.

343 x 183 cm. (11 ft. 3 in. x 6 ft.) Victoria and Albert Museum, London.

20

20. KNOTTED WOOLEN CARPET (FRAGMENT); TURKISH COURT MANUFACTURE, 16TH CENTURY

In the field are cartouches with naturalistic flowers (carnations, tulips, hyacinths) and palmette-shaped pendants, surrounded by more flowers and foliage and separated by the lobed ends of another medallion system outlined in white. The border is of giant flowers and cloud bands. Carnations, tulips, and hyacinths are among the favorite flower motifs of the Turkish carpet.

436 x 248 cm. (14 ft. 4 in. x 8 ft. 2 in.) Warp and weft silk. Sehna or Persian knot, 195 knots per sq. in. Österreichisches Museum für angewandte Kunst, Vienna.

22

23

**21. KNOTTED WOOLEN CARPET; TURKISH COURT
MANUFACTURE, CA. 1600**

Against a dark blue ground, lozenge fields are loosely outlined with
pairs of saw-edged cloud bands enclosing small medallions, the
whole superimposed on a pattern of flowering scrolls; the principal
border is also filled with scrolls. The scroll guard stripes are identical.
415 x 287 cm. (13 ft. 8 in. x 9 ft. 5 in.) Ghiordes or Turkish knot, approx.
410 knots per sq. in. Formerly in Islamic section, Staatliche Museen, Berlin.
Destroyed by fire, 1945.

**22. KNOTTED WOOLEN CARPET; ANATOLIAN,
17TH CENTURY**

On the white ground are wavy cloud bands with a triangular
arrangement of spheres (the *Chintamani* pattern of the Chinese).
The principal border contains arabesque-like cloud bands; the guard
stripes, stiff scrolling stems. A characteristic Anatolian seventeenth-
century border. (See *Ill. 23*.)
339 x 220 cm. (11 ft. 2 in. x 7 ft. 3 in.) Museo Bardini, Florence.

**23. KNOTTED WOOLEN CARPET ("BIRD CARPET");
ANATOLIAN, 17TH CENTURY**

On the white ground rosettes are linked by birdlike, angular leaves—
to which this type of carpet owes its name—between groups of
flowers. In the border cloud bands and flowering scrolls form
arabesques.
380 x 186 cm. (12 ft. 6 in. x 6 ft. 1 in.) From a private collection in Vienna.

24. PRAYER RUG; ANATOLIAN, 17TH CENTURY

The field is light red. In the spandrels are carnations with large saw-edged leaves. The cross panel is filled with bunches of flowers. The border consists of large rosettes, *herati,* carnations, and hyacinths. The continuous scroll (*Pl. II and Ill. 14*) has been broken up into separate components.

160 x 120 cm. (5 ft. 3 in. x 3 ft. 11 in.) 100 knots per sq. in. Österreichisches Museum für angewandte Kunst, Vienna.

25

25. PRAYER RUG; ANATOLIAN, 17TH CENTURY

The field consists of a tripartite mihrab on a white ground. Above the gable appear two pairs of curved, saw-edged leaves, each enclosing a rosette; the cross panel contains tulips. In the principal border hexagons enclose small lozenges with radiating flowers; guard stripes are of lattice. With its columns, the decoration above the gable, and the cross panel, this piece is a forerunner of the so-called Pillar Ladik. 170 x 120 cm. (5 ft. 7 in. x 3 ft. 11 in.) Österreichisches Museum für angewandte Kunst, Vienna.

26. KNOTTED WOOLEN RUG; ANATOLIAN, 17TH CENTURY

In the white field a lozenge-shaped medallion encloses a hexagon, and the latter in turn encloses a star. The outline of the medallion is formed by rosettes and carnations. In the corners appear large flower-heads and leaves. The border—of a type revived in the Kis-Ghiordes rugs of the nineteenth century—is broken up into triangles of various colors, separated by broad white bands strewn with flowers.

168 x 132 cm. (5 ft. 6 in. x 4 ft. 4 in.) The property of a Viennese dealer.

27. PRAYER RUG; ANATOLIAN, 17TH CENTURY

A tripartite mihrab on a white field. Above the gable, a close network of arabesques is surmounted by carnations and tulips. The cross panels above and below the mihrab are filled with flowering scrolls; the border contains a scrolling stem with rosettes, palmettes, lanceolate leaves, and hyacinths. Guard stripes are also tripartite. As in the example in *Ill. 24,* the border is still reminiscent of the magnificent flowering scrolls of the carpets of Turkish Court manufacture (*Pl. II and Ill. 14*).

180 x 127 cm. (5 ft. 11 in. x 4 ft. 2 in.) Approx. 120 knots per sq. in. Österreichisches Museum für angewandte Kunst, Vienna.

28. PRAYER RUG; KULA, EARLY 19TH CENTURY

The mihrab and spandrels are filled with rows of small flower-heads (*sinekli*); in the two cross panels are giant carnations. The border, though consisting of many narrow bands of equal width (*shobokli*), preserves the tripartite division into principal and guard stripes. Colors in the border are white, green, and a brown approaching black.

175 x 125 cm. (5 ft. 9 in. x 4 ft. 1 in.) Approx. 100 knots per sq. in. Österreichisches Museum für angewandte Kunst, Vienna.

26

27

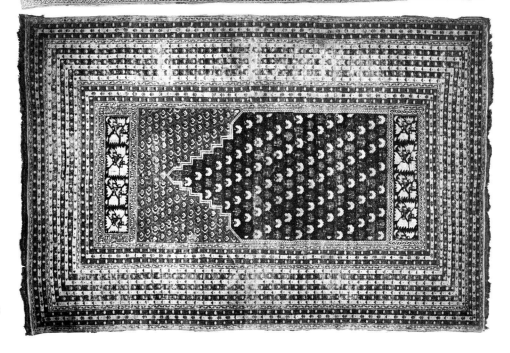

28

PERSIA

Carpets of Persian Court manufacture are always based on individual designs. The shape of medallion and pendant, the in-filling pattern, the decoration of field and border, are never repeated. Standardization does not occur until later.

29. KNOTTED WOOLEN CARPET (FRAGMENT); PERSIAN COURT MANUFACTURE, FIRST HALF 16TH CENTURY

A sixteen-lobed medallion, with two pendants, encloses an eight-pointed star. Flowering scrolls run across the outlines of the lobes. In the rest of the field are thin spiral scrolls. Two entwined systems of band arabesques form the main border. In the three inner guard stripes are small scrolls on the outside gadroons. Medallions of such dominating importance are only found in Persian carpets.
604 x 396 cm. (19 ft. 10 in. x 13 ft.) Victorian and Albert Museum, London.

30. KNOTTED WOOLEN CARPET WITH MEDALLION AND HUNTING SCENES; PERSIAN COURT MANUFACTURE, 1542/43

A sixteen-lobed red medallion with scrolls, long-legged birds, and cloud bands has an inscription at its center. Within the wide pendant are fishes and ducks. Quarter medallions appear at the corner. The dark blue field is filled with hunting scenes and scattered flowers with birds peering out from behind the larger blossoms. The border contains two systems of arabesque bands, one dark blue and one light, and palmettes on a red ground. The inscription reads: "This carpet that moves us by its great beauty was made by Ghiyat uddin-e Djani in the year 949." Field and medallion speak a completely different language.
570 x 365 cm (18 ft. 9 in. x 12 ft.) Museo Poldi-Pezzoli, Milan.

31. FRAGMENT OF A KNOTTED WOOLEN CARPET; PERSIAN COURT MANUFACTURE, FIRST HALF 16TH CENTURY

Against a yellow field appears a beautiful landscape with cypresses, flowering trees, wild animals, and birds. The red medallion has a saw-edged black outline and contains flowering branches and birds. In the red border are animals and birds amid giant flower-heads, scrolls, and clouds.
350 x 410 cm. (11 ft. 6 in. x 13 ft. 5 in.) Musée des arts décoratifs, Paris.

32

32. FRAGMENT OF A KNOTTED WOOLEN CARPET; PERSIAN COURT MANUFACTURE, FIRST HALF 16TH CENTURY

A large, oval medallion (red) is decorated with long-legged birds and clouds. In the white field is a landscape with cypresses, flower- and fruit-bearing trees, and all kinds of animals, including dragons, chi-lins, and phoenixes; in the corner pieces are winged genii. The dark blue border contains calligraphic arabesques with flowers and spiral scrolls. The fragment shown here was burned during World War II. An identical carpet in the Clarence Mackay Collection, Long Island, is proof that important pieces were often made in pairs.
Formerly in Islamic section, Staatliche Museen, Berlin.

33. KNOTTED WOOLEN CARPET; PERSIAN COURT MANUFACTURE, FIRST HALF 16TH CENTURY

The almost circular center medallion and the pendants are filled with a network of delicate scrolls. The yellow field is covered by a mass of thin, scrolling stems ending in broad arabesques, cloud bands, and gaily colored peacocks. In the principal border, on a red ground, are pairs of spiral scrolls, cloud bands, and small flowers; the guard stripes, too, contain cloud bands.
802 x 412 cm. (26 ft. 4 in. x 13 ft. 6 in.) Courtesy of the Metropolitan Museum of Art, New York. Gift of the Samuel H. Kress Foundation, 1946.

33

34

114

35

34. KNOTTED WOOLEN CARPET; PERSIAN COURT MANUFACTURE, DATED 1539/40

A sixteen-pointed star with the same number of almond-shaped pendants encloses arabesques and cloud bands. There are two lamp pendants besides. Scrolls spread over the dark blue field. The border consists of a succession of arabesque-filled panels, some round, some oblong; in the guard stripes we find arabesques, scrolling stems, and cloud bands. The inscription reads: "I have no refuge in the world other than thy threshold. There is no place of protection for my head other than this door. The work of the slave of the threshold, Maqsud of Kashan, in the year 946." One of the world's most famous carpets, this one comes from the mosque of Ardebil, the burial place of Shah Ismail. Because of its intended use in a mosque, it contains no representations of animals or human beings.

1152 x 534 cm. (37 ft. 9 in. x 17 ft. 6 in.) 340 knots per sq. in. Victoria and Albert Museum, London.

35. SILK CARPET WITH SILVER BROCADING; PERSIAN COURT MANUFACTURE, FIRST HALF 16TH CENTURY

The lobed medallion, within a circle of scrolling stems, is developed from a square, each side of which forms the base of a rectangle containing a peacock. In the field are spiral scrolls with broad arabesque ends. In the border, calligraphic panels alternate with arabesques, the whole being surrounded by cloud bands. Guard stripes consist of flowering scrolls.

250 x 170 cm. (8 ft. 2 in. x 5 ft. 7 in.) Musée des arts décoratifs, Paris.

36

36. KNOTTED WOOLEN CARPET WITH GOLD AND SILVER BROCADING; PERSIAN COURT MANUFACTURE, FIRST HALF 16TH CENTURY

A dark blue medallion with flowering scrolls and birds is centered in the red field. Above and below it, kneeling genii flank a vase; elsewhere appear large trees, wild animals, dragons, bears, and birds. In the light green border is a broad arabesque with animals in pursuit, and animal heads and furs within palmettes. According to the inscription, which, above all, praises the artist's work: "It is like a garden . . . a tulip field . . . a dewy rose . . . spread out on the path of the king of the world." The carpet was in all probability intended for Shah Tahmasp (1524–67).

505 x 240 cm. (16 ft. 7 in. x 7 ft. 11 in.) Sehna or Persian knot, 360 knots per sq. in. Museo Poldi-Pezzoli, Milan.

37. KNOTTED WOOLEN CARPET WITH GOLD AND SILVER BROCADING; PERSIAN COURT MANUFACTURE, SECOND HALF 16TH CENTURY

A lobed medallion with flared outline and arabesques is surrounded by a field of flowering scrolls, giant flower-heads, cloud bands, birds, and dragons. In the border are flowers and panels with inscriptions.

233 x 163 cm. (7 ft. 8 in. x 5 ft. 4 in.) Victoria and Albert Museum, London.

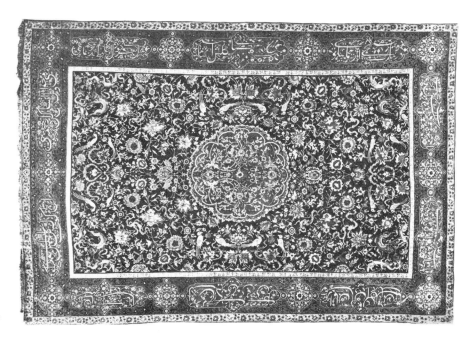

37

38. KNOTTED WOOLEN CARPET; PERSIAN COURT MANUFACTURE, FIRST HALF 16TH CENTURY

The large red medallion in the center contains a network of arabesques and flowering trees surrounding a duck pond; cypresses and flowering trees, wild animals, phoenixes, and small birds fill the dark blue field. The border consists of a reciprocal pattern of red and white lobes with flowering scrolls, birds, and cloud bands. In theme, the medallion contrasts sharply with the rest of the field.

570 x 270 cm. (18 ft. 9 in. x 8 ft. 10 in.) Prince Schwarzenberg, Vienna.

39

39. KNOTTED WOOLEN CARPET; PERSIAN COURT MANUFACTURE, CA. 1600

A red star medallion has deer and panther at its center; in the outer zone are phoenixes and dragons; the pendants contain bears. Against the dark blue field appears a landscape with cypresses and small pools, animals, hunters, and birds, the whole being surrounded by a main border (red) of scrolling stems with giant flower-heads, dragons, and phoenixes. This carpet was at one time in the church of Notre Dame in Mantes.

783 x 379 cm. (25 ft. 8 in. x 12 ft. 5 in.) Musée du Louvre, Paris.

40. KNOTTED WOOLEN CARPET; NORTHWEST PERSIA, LATE 16TH CENTURY

On the dark blue ground are a number of fields of various shapes and colors, arranged in a star pattern. Superimposed in the middle, as a third layer in the composition, is a medallion of eight red and eight white lobes filled with flowering scrolls. In the border are two intersecting systems of wide arabesque bands and giant flower-heads. In the treatment of the field, this carpet resembles the one in *Ill. 43;* the medallion resembles that in *Ill. 29.* That this carpet nevertheless differs from both the others is proof of the infinite versatility of the art of the Persian carpet.

737 x 370 cm. (24 ft. 2 in. x 12 ft. 1 in.) Österreichisches Museum für angewandte Kunst, Vienna.

40

41. SILK RUG; PERSIAN COURT MANUFACTURE, 16TH CENTURY

Quatrefoil medallion and corner pieces are filled with arabesques and flower-heads. In the field we find flowering scrolls, leaves, and clouds. The border contains palmettes and delicate scrolling.
250 x 150 cm. (8 ft. 2 in. x 4 ft. 11 in.) Musée des Gobelins, Paris.

42. KNOTTED WOOLEN CARPET WITH MEDALLION PATTERN; PERSIAN COURT MANUFACTURE, FIRST HALF 16TH CENTURY

The field here is divided into two equal parts, each containing a medallion linked with four pendants to the adjoining half or quarter. Within the medallions are arabesques, flowering scrolls, and birds; above and below them are peacock vases on dragon bases, supported by lions. In the rest of the field appear various trees, and also animals in pursuit; at the center of the carpet is a small fishpond. The reciprocal border is decorated with dragons, phoenixes, cloud bands, and scrolls.
549 x 300 cm. (18 ft. x 10 ft.) Warp and weft silk. Approx. 470 knots per sq. in. Victoria and Albert Museum, London.

42

43. KNOTTED WOOLEN CARPET; PERSIAN COURT MANUFACTURE, FIRST HALF 16TH CENTURY

A design of loosely grouped medallions of various shapes, enclosing dragons, phoenixes, mythical animals, birds, and arabesques, covers the ivory field. Between the medallions are thin, flowering scrolls. The border consists of dark blue panels on a red ground, filled mainly with flowering scrolls.

498 x 340 cm. (16 ft. 4 in. x 11 ft. 2 in.) Courtesy of the Metropolitan Museum of Art, New York. Hewett Fund, 1910.

44. KNOTTED WOOLEN CARPET; SOUTHWEST PERSIA (?), 17TH CENTURY (SO-CALLED PORTUGUESE CARPET)

The red flared medallion at the center is extended by broad bands (yellow, dark blue, light blue, green, yellow) with similarly agitated outlines as far as the border on the right and left. Medallion and bands are filled with flowers and birds. In the four corners of the white field are sailing ships with European and native crews; two men can be seen raising themselves out of the water. In the red border are wide, dark blue arabesques (see also the dust jacket of this volume). This carpet is the finest example of its type, whose origins and significance are still a matter of dispute.

677 x 372 cm. (22 ft. 3 in. x 12 ft. 3 in.) Warp and weft cotton. Ghiordes or Turkish knot, a strange feature in a carpet seemingly Persian. 310 knots per sq. in. Österreichisches Museum für angewandte Kunst, Vienna.

44

45. KNOTTED WOOLEN CARPET; NORTHWEST PERSIA, 17TH CENTURY

The star-shaped medallion, filled with small flowering branches and animals, is set in a white field covered with a pattern of arabesques. In the corners, simplified medallion quarters form a gable, a motif which recurs in the Tabriz carpets of the nineteenth century. The border is of reciprocal lobes filled with flowers.

635 x 330 cm. (20 ft. 10 in. x 10 ft. 10 in.) Österreichisches Museum für angewandte Kunst, Vienna.

46

46. KNOTTED WOOLEN CARPET WITH BROCADING;
PERSIAN COURT MANUFACTURE, MIDDLE 16TH CENTURY

This is the so-called Metropolitan animal carpet. Animals, some in combat, are spaced about on the red field, surrounded by flowering scrolls. The horizontal axis is not in the exact middle, and some of the pattern therefore remains incomplete. The border is filled with arabesques and cloud bands.

325 x 175 cm. (10 ft. 8 in. x 5 ft. 9 in.) Approx. 570 knots per sq. in. Courtesy of the Metropolitan Museum of Art, New York. Hewitt Fund, 1910.

48

47. KNOTTED SILK CARPET; PERSIAN COURT MANUFACTURE, MIDDLE 16TH CENTURY

The red field contains both mythical and natural animals, some in combat, against a background of flowering trees and plants. The dark green border consists of giant flower-heads flanked by birds.
228 x 179 cm. (7 ft. 6 in. x 5 ft. 10 in.) Courtesy of the Metropolitan Museum of Art, New York. Bequest of Benjamin Altmann, 1913.

48. KNOTTED WOOLEN CARPET; PERSIAN COURT MANUFACTURE, SECOND HALF 16TH CENTURY

The landscape, indicated by leaves and flowering plants, is filled with hunting scenes and scenes from famous Persian love stories—Chosroes discovering Shirin bathing, Laila finding the dying Majnun. In the border are giant flower-heads, genii within lobed fields, large lanceolate leaves, and animals in combat. The pattern of the carpet is not completely symmetrical and integrated. A new set of scenes begins below the phoenixes. Narrative carpets are extremely rare in Oriental art.
375 x 270 cm. (12 ft. 3 in. x 8 ft. 10 in.) Musée des arts décoratifs, Paris.

49

49. KNOTTED WOOLEN CARPET (FRAGMENT); PERSIAN COURT MANUFACTURE, MIDDLE 16TH CENTURY

On the red ground are giant flower-heads, cloud bands, and animals amid scrolling stems; in the white border are large palmettes and wide arabesques, linked by scrolling stems and cloud bands.

183 x 126 cm. (6 ft. x 4 ft. 2 in.) Warp and weft silk. 320 knots per sq. in. Österreichisches Museum für angewandte Kunst, Vienna.

50

50. KNOTTED WOOLEN CARPET; PERSIAN COURT
MANUFACTURE, MIDDLE 16TH CENTURY

In an almost invisible scroll network, giant flower-heads, animals in
pursuit or combat, dragons, birds, and cloud bands embellish the red
field. The dark green border contains spiral scrolls with flowers and
cloud bands. The inner guard stripe bears an inscription which praises
the carpet and blesses the Shah.

760 x 325 cm. (24 ft. 11 in. x 10 ft. 8 in.) Warp and weft silk. 310 knots per
sq. in. Österreichisches Museum für angewandte Kunst, Vienna.

51

52

**51. KNOTTED WOOLEN RUG; EASTERN PERSIA (?),
POSSIBLY HERAT, CA. 1600**

Giant flower-heads on thin spiral scrolls and a profusion of cloud
bands and birds cover the field. The border, too, contains spiral scrolls
and giant flower-heads. The scroll network in this example is closer
and more Chinese in character.

224 x 207 cm. (7 ft. 4 in. x 6 ft. 9 in.) Victoria and Albert Museum, London.

**52. KNOTTED WOOLEN CARPET; EASTERN PERSIA (?),
CA. 1600**

Giant flower-heads and lanceolate leaves on pairs of scrolling stems
fill the field, and a different arrangement of similar motifs makes
up the main border.

410 x 175 cm. (13 ft. 5 in. x 5 ft. 8 in.) Courtesy of the Metropolitan Museum
of Art, New York. Bequest of Benjamin Altmann, 1913.

53. KNOTTED WOOLEN CARPET; PERSIAN COURT MANUFACTURE, FIRST HALF 17TH CENTURY

Boldly curved, scrolling stems ending in large lanceolate leaves are interspersed with giant flower-heads and flowering branches on the red ground. In the narrow blue border are more flower-heads and scrolls. Some authorities believe the flowering branches establish a link with the so-called vase carpets.
265 x 195 cm. (8 ft. 9 in. x 6 ft. 5 in.) Corcoran Art Gallery, Washington, D.C. The W. A. Clark Collection.

54. KNOTTED WOOLEN RUG; NORTHWEST PERSIA, 17TH CENTURY

In the field are spiral scrolls with arabesques, flowers, and almost angular cloud bands. The border contains panels and stylized flowers. Plant motifs now seem frozen into rigidity.
220 x 128 cm. (7 ft. 2 in. x 4 ft. 3 in.) Formerly in Islamic section, Staatliche Museen, Berlin.

55. KNOTTED WOOLEN CARPET; PERSIAN COURT MANUFACTURE, 16TH CENTURY

Three overlapping systems of scrolling stems with giant flower-heads and vases spread over the field, augmented by flowering branches. In the border are additional flower-heads and scrolling stems; in the guard stripes, scrolls and diaper fields. This carpet can be considered the archetype of all vase carpets, none of which surpasses it in workmanship and clarity of design.
519 x 330 cm. (17 ft. x 10 ft. 9 in.) Victoria and Albert Museum, London.

54

55

56. KNOTTED WOOLEN CARPET; NORTHWEST PERSIA, CA. 1600

The field contains a system of intersecting scrolls with diamond-shaped medallions at the points of intersection. Stylized giant flower-heads and vaselike forms, as well as an abundance of small flowers, fill in the ground. In the narrow border—a characteristic feature of most vase carpets—appear giant flower-heads and lanceolate leaves on scrolling stems.

747 x 287 cm. (24 ft. 6 in. x 9 ft. 5 in.) Victoria and Albert Museum, London.

57. KNOTTED WOOLEN CARPET; NORTHWEST PERSIA, CA. 1600

On the green ground are rows of vaselike shapes with flowering branches. The border contains a garland of forked leaves with naturalistic and stylized flowers; the guard stripes, small scrolling stems.

610 x 255 cm. (20 ft. x 8 ft. 4 in.) Österreichisches Museum für angewandte Kunst, Vienna.

58

58. KNOTTED WOOLEN CARPET; NORTHWEST PERSIA OR CAUCASUS, CA. 1600

A number of small fields of various colors, formed in part by a net-work of scrolls, covers the ground. Within these fields are vases, fruits resembling berries, large flower-heads, and flowering branches. Rows of flowers make up the narrow border. It has not yet been established whether carpets of this type are Persian or Caucasian.
480 x 385 cm. (15 ft. 9 in. x 12 ft. 7 in.) Formerly in Tschinili Kösk, Istanbul.

59. KNOTTED WOOLEN CARPET (FRAGMENT); NORTHWEST PERSIA, 17TH CENTURY

A closely grouped arrangement of intersecting rectangles distin-guishes this example, which represents a highly original develop-ment of the vase carpet. Only the fields in every other row are of the same color; the ground between also is not uniform. Eight colors are used in all. They form a lively mosaic pattern under a network of scrolling stems supporting stylized flower-heads. The simple border contains a wavy scroll.
487 x 275 cm. (15 ft. 11 in. x 9 ft.) Courtesy of the Metropolitan Museum of Art. New York. Bequest of Horace Havemeyer, 1950.

59

60. KNOTTED WOOLEN CARPET; CENTRAL PERSIA, 17TH CENTURY

The large, somewhat coarse, flowers flanked by lanceolate leaves are a characteristic feature of these carpets. The scrolling stems almost disappear. In the border are similar motifs.

513 x 210 cm. (16 ft. 10 in. x 6 ft. 11 in.) Baroness von Essen, Skokloster, Sweden.

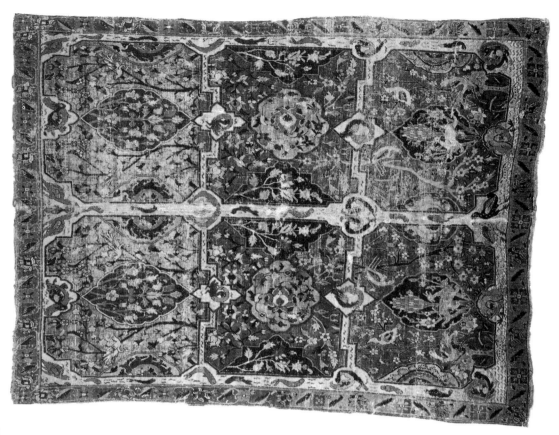

61

61. GARDEN RUG, WOOL WITH GOLD AND SILVER BROCADING; NORTHWEST PERSIA OR CAUCASUS, CA. 1600

The red ground is divided into six fields by canals, which widen in places and carry fish and ducks. Each field contains a center medallion flanked by half-medallions, and also flowering trees, birds, deer, and flowering scrolls. In the narrow border is a scrolling stem with diagonal leaves, flowers, and rosettes.

187 x 151 cm. (6 ft. 1 in. x 4 ft. 11 in.) Österreichisches Museum für angewandte Kunst, Vienna.

62

136

63

62. GARDEN CARPET; NORTHWEST PERSIA, 18TH CENTURY

The division of the field here into land and water is not very strict; the same small trees appear in both. There is a reciprocal trefoil border.

310 x 178 cm. (10 ft. 2 in. x 5 ft. 10 in.) Formerly in Islamic section, Staatliche Museen, Berlin.

63. KNOTTED WOOLEN CARPET; NORTHWEST PERSIA OR CAUCASUS, FIRST HALF 17TH CENTURY

The field contains several rows of flowering shrubs; the border, two intersecting systems of arabesques and flowering scrolls.

272 x 178 cm. (8 ft. 11 in. x 5 ft. 10 in.) Courtesy of the Metropolitan Museum of Art, New York. Gift of James F. Ballard, 1922.

64

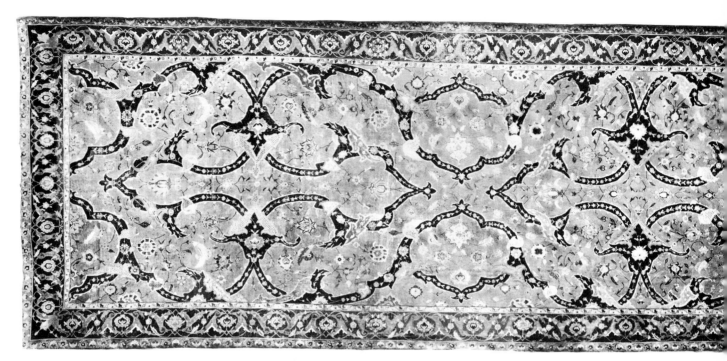

65

64. KNOTTED WOOLEN CARPET; PERSIAN, 16TH CENTURY

On the red ground appears a landscape of cypresses, flowering trees, and shrubs, arranged in three rows. In the border are three systems of arabesques (red, blue, and yellow); in the guard stripes, flowering scrolls.

525 x 329 cm. (17 ft. 2 in. x 10 ft. 9 in.) Museum of Art (C. F. William Collection), Philadelphia.

65. KNOTTED WOOLEN CARPET; PERSIAN COURT MANUFACTURE, 16TH CENTURY

On the red ground flowering scrolls and wide arabesques with small flowers are interwoven. The border contains arabesques, scrolling stems, and split leaves.

790 x 315 cm. (25 ft. 11 in. x 10 ft. 4 in.) Corcoran Art Gallery, Washington, D.C. W. A. Clark Collection.

**66. PRAYER RUG, WOOL WITH BROCADING; PERSIAN,
16TH CENTURY**

The mihrab is filled with large cloud bands and flowering scrolls.
In the small panel is an inscription praising Allah. The border, on
a yellow ground, contains flowering scrolls and arabesques in the
lower half. The upper half, like the spandrels, contains inscriptions
from the Koran. The guard stripes are of wavy scrolls. This rug is
related to the products of Persian Court manufacture in character.
161 x 107 cm. (5 ft. 3 in. x 3 ft. 6 in.) 625 knots per sq. in. Courtesy of the
Metropolitan Museum of Art, New York. Bequest of Isaac D. Fletscher, 1917.

67

67. WOOLEN PRAYER RUG; PERSIAN, 16TH CENTURY

The bluish-green mihrab has flowering trees, and above the cloud
bands a vase with flowering branches. In the red spandrels is a network of arabesques. The border panels are filled with arabesques
(below) and inscriptions in praise of Allah and the Prophets (above).
164 x 100 cm. (5 ft. 5 in. x 3 ft. 4 in.) Courtesy of the Metropolitan Museum
of Art, New York. Bequest of Benjamin Altmann, 1913.

68

POLONAISE CARPETS

The following pages illustrate brocaded silk carpets of the first half of the seventeenth century, known as Polonaise carpets in the past but now usually called Shah Abbas carpets. They bear all the characteristics of a Court product (individual design) and in their more grandiose, almost Baroque patterns reflect the general trend of the age. They are comparatively loosely knotted (155 to 220 knots per sq. in.) and often lavishly brocaded in gold and silver.

68. BROCADED SILK CARPET; PERSIAN COURT MANUFACTURE, FIRST HALF 17TH CENTURY

The carpet is filled with a pattern of cloud bands and flowering scrolls. In the border a scrolling stem with large palmettes is flanked by arabesques. This carpet is still used in the coronation of the Kings of Denmark.

520 x 370 cm. (17 ft. 1 in. x 12 ft. 2 in.) Rosenborg Castle, Copenhagen.

**69. BROCADED SILK RUG; PERSIAN COURT
MANUFACTURE, FIRST HALF 17TH CENTURY**

From the middle of the brown field a large medallion extends
almost to the corners. Flowering scrolls and arabesques spread across
medallion and field, regardless of dividing outlines. The border is
reciprocal trefoil.

200 x 138 cm. (6 ft. 7 in. x 4 ft. 6 in.) Prince Liechtenstein, Vaduz.

**70. BROCADED SILK RUG; PERSIAN COURT
MANUFACTURE, FIRST HALF 17TH CENTURY**

The octagonal star medallion has radiating flowering shoots which
further divide the field. In the guard stripe is a reciprocal trefoil
pattern. Here a clear distinction between medallion and field has
been dispensed with.

210 x 143 cm. (6 ft. 11 in x 4 ft. 8 in.) Formerly in Islamic section, Staatliche
Museen, Berlin.

*Because of their designs, woven silk carpets can be considered
products of Persian Court manufacture.*

69

70

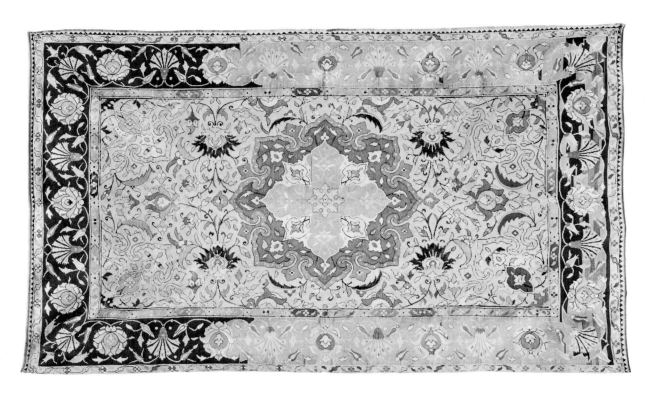

**71. WOVEN SILK RUG; PERSIAN,
FIRST HALF OF 17TH CENTURY**

A lobed star-shaped medallion encloses a rhombus, and within the latter is a cross. Tiny medallion quarters appear in the corners; the rest of the field is covered with flowering scrolls. The border contains a scrolling stem with large stylized flower-heads, carnations, and tulips; the guard stripes, wavy scrolls.
200 x 138 cm. (6 ft. 7 in. x 4 ft. 6 in.) Courtesy of the Metropolitan Museum of Art, New York. Gift of Horace Havemeyer, 1951.

**72. WOVEN SILK RUG; PERSIAN,
EARLY 17TH CENTURY**

At the center appear the arms of Sigismund (III) Vasa, King of Poland, set within a rectangular pendant medallion. The corners contain quarter medallions with arabesques; the rest of the field, flowering scrolls. The border is of palmettes, lanceolate leaves, and rosettes.
250 x 135 cm. (8 ft. 2 in. x 4 ft. 5 in.) Residenzmuseum, Munich.

72

73

148

CAUCASUS

All the Persian motifs live on in Caucasian carpets, but they have become coarser and larger, and almost seem to swamp the disproportionately narrow border.

73. KNOTTED WOOLEN CARPET; CAUCASIAN, CA. 1600

Saw-edged leaves divide the ground into diamond-shaped fields enclosing giant flower-heads, stylized animal combats, and berries on stiff stems. Some of the detail is inspired by contemporary Persian carpets. Large flower-heads and lanceolate leaves form the border, which—characteristic of Caucasian carpets and rugs—is comparatively narrow and consists of only one stripe.

678 x 230 cm. (22 ft. 3 in. x 7 ft. 6 in.) Formerly in Islamic section, Staatliche Museen, Berlin.

74. KNOTTED WOOLEN CARPET; CAUCASIAN, 17TH CENTURY

The large palmette-shaped fields with giant flower-heads, linked by thin scrolls across the dark blue ground, are a development of the main feature of the Persian vase carpet. Borders of diagonal saw-edged leaves have retained their popularity in some parts of the Caucasus until the present day.

298 x 167 cm. (9 ft. 9 in. x 5 ft. 6 in.) Ghiordes or Turkish knot, 120 knots per sq. in. Österreichisches Museum für angewandte·Kunst, Vienna.

75

75. KNOTTED WOOLEN CARPET; CAUCASIAN, 17TH CENTURY

Stripes and pairs of wide saw-edged leaves divide the ground into lozenge-shaped fields enclosing giant flower-heads and animals in combat. The border is of reciprocal trefoils.

452 x 202 cm. (14 ft. 10 in. x 6 ft. 7 in.) Ghiordes or Turkish knot, 75 knots per sq. in. Österreichisches Museum für angewandte Kunst, Vienna.

76. KNOTTED WOOLEN CARPET; CAUCASIAN, CA. 1700

The bands between the lozenge-shaped fields have become wider, the giant flower-heads and groups of animals in combat, edged with hook motifs, even more stylized. In the border are rosettes, stiff leaves, and S-forms.

373 x 168 cm. (12 ft. 3 in. x 5 ft. 6 in.) Formerly in Islamic section, Staatliche Museen, Berlin. Destroyed by fire in 1945.

**77. KNOTTED WOOLEN CARPET; CAUCASIAN,
18TH CENTURY**

This narrow carpet shows only incomplete lozenge-shaped fields. Within the smaller fields are giant flower-heads; in the larger half-lozenges are stiff, flowering tendrils. The border contains wavy tendrils.

470 x 233 cm. (15 ft. 5 in. x 7 ft. 8 in.) Museum of Art, Philadelphia.

78. KNOTTED WOOLEN CARPET; CAUCASIAN, CA. 1600

Against a red ground, stiff stems with arabesque leaves are set amid giant flower-heads, rosettes, and bell-shaped flowers. In the border are diagonal leaves and large flower-heads. This pattern continues into the nineteenth century.

465 x 195 cm. (15 ft. 3 in. x 6 ft. 5 in.) Ghiordes or Turkish knot, 60 to 65 knots per sq. in. Österreichisches Museum für angewandte Kunst, Vienna.

79. KNOTTED WOOLEN CARPET; CAUCASIAN, 17TH CENTURY

On the red ground is a pattern of widely spaced stars, with large flower-heads, pairs of leaves, and zigzag lines. A flowering, scrolling stem forms the border.

379 x 207 cm. (12 ft. x 6 ft. 9 in.) Ghiordes or Turkish knot, 85 to 90 knots per sq. in. Österreichisches Museum für angewandte Kunst, Vienna.

80. KNOTTED WOOLEN RUG; CAUCASIAN, CA. 1700

Giant flower-heads, lanceolate leaves, and very thin scrolling stems cover a dark blue field which is framed by a wavy scroll border with tulip-heads.

226 x 175 cm. (7 ft. 5 in. x 5 ft. 9 in.) Österreichisches Museum für angewandte Kunst, Vienna.

79

80

81. KNOTTED WOOLEN CARPET (FRAGMENT), CAUCASIAN, 17TH CENTURY

Under a network of flowering tendrils appear broad stiff stems, with giant flower-heads at the points of intersection and large bell-shaped flowers flanked by saw-edged leaves. Arabesque and flowering scroll form the border.
Formerly in Islamic section, Staatliche Museen, Berlin.

81

82. KNOTTED WOOLEN CARPET; CAUCASIAN, 17TH/18TH CENTURY

Three rows of fields of various shapes are filled with flowers; the rest of the ground is covered with flower- and fruit-bearing trees. This carpet is based on those of the golden age of Persian carpets (see *Pl. V*). In the border are diagonal leaves and flowers.
490 x 272 cm. (16 ft. 1 in. x 8 ft. 11 in.) Museum of Art, Philadelphia.

82

83. KNOTTED WOOLEN CARPET; CAUCASIAN, 18TH CENTURY

Oval medallions, each with four radiating saw-edged, lanceolate leaves, are set between smaller medallions and stiff flowering stems, inside a wavy scroll border.

370 x 178 cm. (12 ft. 1 in. x 5 ft. 10 in.) Musée des arts décoratifs, Paris.

84. KNOTTED WOOLEN CARPET; CAUCASIAN, 18TH CENTURY

A pattern of large bell-shaped flowers and angular saw-edged leaves is set within a border of two kinds of flowering shrubs.

465 x 210 cm. (15 ft. 3 in. x 6 ft. 10 in.) Formerly in the Hollitscher Collection, Berlin.

84

157

85

INDIA

In its patterns, the Indian carpet resembles the Persian, though there is a preference for not only naturalistic animals but also plants.

85. KNOTTED WOOLEN CARPET (FRAGMENT); PERSIAN OR INDIAN, CA. 1500

On the dark ground are large spiral scrolls with animal heads and flowers; the border is of arabesques. A miniature by the Persian painter Behzad, dated 1467, showing Timur giving an audience, displays a similar motif on the tent roof.
147 x 105 cm. (4 ft. 10 in. x 3 ft. 5 in.) Musée des arts décoratifs, Paris.

86. WOOLEN PRAYER RUG; INDIAN, 17TH CENTURY

The red field under the yellow arch is filled with a variety of flowers, all growing from one small shrub which rises from the little blue mound at the base between the two cypresses. The tripartite main border stripe is dark green, with flowering scrolls. The scroll guard stripes are also tripartite.
155 x 107 cm. (5 ft. 1 in. x 3 ft. 6 in.) Warp and weft silk. Sehna or Persian knot, approx. 420 knots per sq. in. Österreichisches Museum für angewandte Kunst, Vienna.

87

87. KNOTTED WOOLEN CARPET; INDIAN, 17TH CENTURY

On the red ground is an all-over pattern of flowers and leaves, partly in a lighter red. The border is of closely spaced panels filled with flowers, and rosettes, set in cloud bands. In the guard stripes are wavy stems and small flowers.

923 x 338 cm. (30 ft. 3 in. x 11 ft. 1 in.) Courtesy of the Metropolitan Museum of Art, New York. Gift of J. Pierpont Morgan, 1917.

88. KNOTTED WOOLEN CARPET; INDIAN, FIRST HALF 17TH CENTURY

The red ground is covered by a pattern of scrolls with giant flower-heads and leaves; among these are square and rectangular medallions. The dark blue border contains naturalistic flowers and shrubs; the guard stripes, scrolls and rosettes.

406 x 167 cm. (13 ft. 4 in. x 5 ft. 6 in.) Sehna or Persian knot, 460 knots per sq. in. Courtesy of the Metropolitan Museum of Art, New York. Bequest of Benjamin Altmann, 1913.

88

159

89

160

90

89. KNOTTED WOOLEN CARPET (FRAGMENT); INDIAN, 17TH CENTURY

Against a red ground a pattern of large flower-heads (seen in profile and from above, in alternate rows) is linked by lanceolate leaves. This design is superimposed on a network of thin scrolls with somewhat smaller flower-heads which form the centers of the lozenge-shaped fields. In the border, trees and flowering shrubs grow from grassy hillocks. This is one of the finest knotted carpets in existence. 294 x 127 cm. (9 ft. 8 in. x 4 ft. 2 in.) Warp and weft silk. Sehna or Persian knot, 1,420 knots per sq. in. Courtesy of the Metropolitan Museum of Art, New York. Bequest of Benjamin Altmann, 1913.

90. KNOTTED WOOLEN CARPET; INDIAN, CA. 1600

The three-tiered landscape—distance being indicated by the size of the trees and birds—is framed by a border of spiral scrolls with giant flower-heads and lion masks.

235 x 156 cm. (7 ft. 10 in. x 5 ft. 1 in.) Sehna or Persian knot, 470 knots per sq. in. Österreichisches Museum für angewandte Kunst, Vienna.

91. KNOTTED WOOLEN RUG; INDIAN, FIRST HALF 17TH CENTURY

The field shows a palace scene, with animals in combat and in pursuit, below. A chained hunting cheetah goes by a bullock cart; a fabulous beast with the winged body of a lion and an elephant's head attacks a small black elephant, and is in turn attacked by a phoenix. Small flowering shrubs indicate a landscape. In the border are palmettes enclosing human and animal heads, set amid birds and flowering scrolls.

243 x 151 cm. (8 ft. x 4 ft. 11 in.) Sehna or Persian knot, 400 knots per sq. in. Courtesy of the Museum of Fine Arts, Boston.

CHINA

Chinese carpets are of more recent origin and therefore form a group apart from the main stream of development.

92. KNOTTED WOOLEN CARPET; CHINESE, 18TH CENTURY

On the white ground are five circular medallions, the middle one filled with peonies. The corners contain large flowering branches; between the medallions are vases, flowering branches, and butterflies. The border is formed by varied meander designs.
187 x 251 cm. (6 ft. 2 in. x 8 ft. 3 in.) Victoria and Albert Museum, London.

92

93. KNOTTED WOOLEN CARPET; CHINESE, 18TH CENTURY

On a pink ground strewn with flowering branches is a large Fu dog surrounded by eight smaller Fu dogs. The border is of peonies on scrolling stems.

280 x 214 cm. (9 ft. 9 in. x 7 ft.) Victoria and Albert Museum, London.

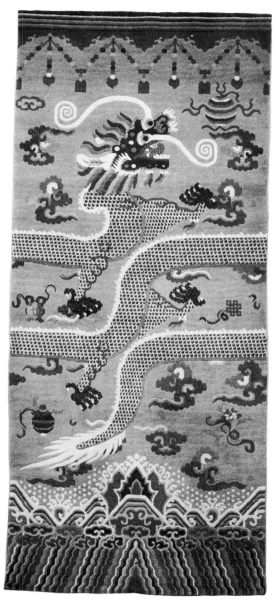

94

94. KNOTTED WOOLEN CARPET; CHINESE, 18TH CENTURY

This carpet is intended to go around a pillar. When it is used in this manner, the ends of the dragon will join. Clouds and symbols of good luck are depicted; at the lower edge are earth and water.

305 x 127 cm. (10 ft. x 4 ft. 2 in.) Warp and weft cotton. Sehna or Persian knot, approx. 35 to 40 knots per sq. in. Österreichisches Museum für angewandte Kunst, Vienna.

95

168

EGYPT

The carpets shown in the following pages, though made in Cairo, were at one time attributed to Damascus. The name "Damascus carpet" is still widely used, particularly in England. Many Continental authorities prefer to speak of two distinct groups, using the term "Mameluke carpet" for specimens with geometric decoration, and "Ottoman carpet" for those with a floral design, since a change of style may in all likelihood have come with the conquest of Cairo by the Ottoman Turks.

95. KNOTTED WOOLEN RUG, MAMELUKE; CAIRO, CA. 1500

In the center of the field is a large octagonal medallion surrounded by small octagons; in the corners are medium-sized octagons filled with an interlacement design. The border contains round and oblong panels filled with small leaves on stiff stems.

188 x 131 cm. (6 ft. 2 in. x 4 ft. 4 in.) Formerly in Islamic section, Staatliche Museen, Berlin.

96. SILK MAMELUKE CARPET; CAIRO, FIRST HALF 16TH CENTURY

The field is covered by a mosaic pattern with three large medallions, the first a green octagon within a blue star; the two others are octagons outlined in blue, green, and red. In between are lozenges, octagons, stars, and narrow bands. Within the medallions and the larger field sections appears a variety of closely-grouped, tiny leaves. The principal border contains red scrolling stems with blue flowers on a green ground, flanked by scroll guard stripes. This carpet is the only known silk one of its kind.

540 x 290 cm. (17 ft. 9 in. x 9 ft. 6 in.) Warp and weft silk. Sehna or Persian knot, 200 to 210 knots per sq. in. Österreichisches Museum für angewandte Kunst, Vienna.

97. KNOTTED WOOLEN RUG; CAIRO, FIRST HALF 16TH CENTURY

A quatrefoil pattern of lanceolate leaves is interspersed by flowering scrolls. In the border are arabesques flanked by tulips and carnations. The guard stripes contain small rosettes. The design is obviously influenced by the products of the Turkish Court manufacture.

221 x 157 cm. (7 ft. 3 in. x 5 ft. 2 in.) Victoria and Albert Museum, London.

97

**98. KNOTTED WOOLEN CARPET, MAMELUKE;
CAIRO, CA. 1500**

On the red ground are yellow octagons within blue stars, surrounded
by smaller octagons. Both field and panel border are covered with
small leaves on stiff stems.
740 x 340 cm. (24 ft. 3 in. x 11 ft. 2 in.) Warp and weft wool. Sehna or
Persian knot, 80 knots per sq. in. Österreichisches Museum für angewandte
Kunst, Vienna.

98

SPAIN

The designs of early Spanish carpets resemble those of Anatolian carpets. Gradually, these were replaced by the Renaissance patterns of contemporary silks and velvets.

99. KNOTTED WOOLEN RUG; SPANISH, 15TH CENTURY

The red field is divided into three rectangles, each enclosing an octagon, and within each octagon a star appears. The rectangles are separated by a pattern of small vases with branches. The border contains star-shaped rosettes. Predominating colors are blue, red, and black.

202 x 120 cm. (6 ft. 7 in. x 3 ft. 11 in.) Warp and weft wool. 100 to 110 knots per sq. in. Victoria and Albert Museum, London.

98

173

**100. KNOTTED WOOLEN CARPET; SPANISH,
15TH CENTURY**

The field is covered by an all-over pattern of octagons, stars, and lozenges, within a calligraphic interlacement border. This carpet bears a particularly close resemblance to Anatolian pieces (see *Ill. 7*).
463 x 206 cm. (15 ft. 2 in. x 6 ft. 9 in.) Museum of Fine Arts, Boston.

**101. KNOTTED WOOLEN RUG; SPANISH,
LATE 15TH CENTURY**

A design of interlacing blue ropes divides the red ground into a series of fields enclosing the thistle flower of the "pomegranate" pattern. The diaper border has stiff stems and a continuous scrolling stem.
229 x 163 cm. (7 ft. 6 in. x 5 ft. 4 in.) Warp and weft wool. 100 to 110 knots per sq. in. Victoria and Albert Museum, London.

**102. KNOTTED WOOLEN CARPET; SPANISH,
16TH CENTURY**

Two rows of octagons filled with arabesques cover the red field. In between are smaller octagons formed by stylized flowers. The border consists of grotesques, with coats-of-arms at the corners.
Courtesy of the Hispanic Society of America, New York.

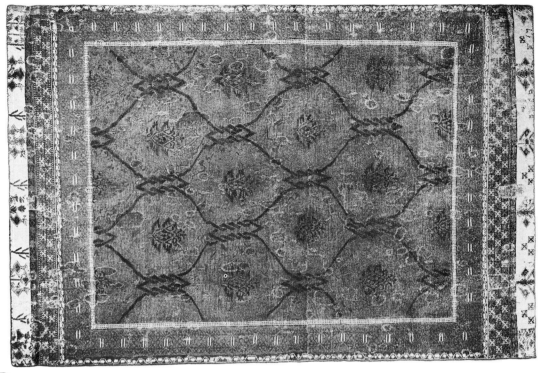

101

102

103

103. KNOTTED WOOLEN RUG; SPANISH, 16TH CENTURY

A plaitwork (braided) band divides the blue ground into small, lozenge-shaped fields, each filled with the "pomegranate" motif. At the center is a square medallion with the Sacred Monogram within a wreath of vases and foliage; above and below, four smaller medallions enclose skulls. In the border are grotesques on a red ground. 290 x 190 cm. (9 ft. 6 in. x 6 ft. 3 in.) Victoria and Albert Museum, London.

104. KNOTTED WOOLEN CARPET; SPANISH, CA. 1600

An all-over design of stylized flower-heads and leaves on scrolling stems forms the so-called "pomegranate" pattern. Wavy scrolls with large leaves fill the border.
Victoria and Albert Museum, London.

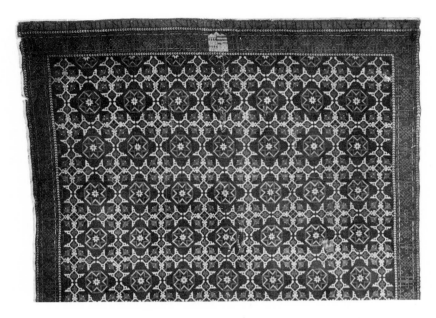

105

ENGLAND

The earliest English carpets were frequently careful copies of Ushak and other Anatolian carpets. Patterned after the floral designs of the seventeenth century, they came to resemble increasingly the products of the French Savonnerie factory.

105. KNOTTED WOOLEN CARPET; ENGLISH, DATED 1603

A small geometric all-over pattern in the manner of fifteenth-century Anatolian rugs, though somewhat simplified, makes up the field. The octagons are linked by arabesques, which, like the motif of the Kufic border, originally represented Arabic characters. At the bottom is the inscription: FEARE GOD AND KEEPE HIS COMMANDMENTS. MADE IN THE YEAR 1603.
Victoria and Albert Museum, London.

106. KNOTTED WOOLEN CARPET; ENGLISH, DATED 1672

The dark blue ground is closely covered with a floral design; at the center appears a coat of arms with lily-crosses, and the date, 1672.
Victoria and Albert Museum, London.

106

FRANCE

France, where the carpet industry was protected against foreign competition by royal decree, was the first country to produce an European Baroque carpet style which lived on until well into the nineteenth century.

107. KNOTTED WOOLEN CARPET; FRENCH (SAVONNERIE), CA. 1700

On the dark brown ground are naturalistic flowers in baskets and cornucopias. The small inner field is framed by a border of tassels and trefoils. From about this time onward, the love of rich floral decoration became very marked throughout the applied arts in practically every country.

247 x 174 cm. (8 ft. 1 in. x 5 ft. 8 in.) Österreichisches Museum für angewandte Kunst, Vienna.

107

109

108. KNOTTED WOOLEN CARPET; FRENCH (SAVONNERIE), END OF 18TH CENTURY

In the central field an oval medallion encloses a shell filled with fruit and surrounded by lyres. Above and below are pairs of chained eagles. The corners contain gardening implements, shepherd's crooks, and the like. This carpet has all the Savonnerie characteristics: bright, well-graduated colors and detail so naturalistic that one almost hesitates to walk on it.

848 x 530 cm. (27 ft. 10 in. x 17 ft. 5 in.) Formerly in Österreichisches Museum für angewandte Kunst, Vienna.

109. KNOTTED WOOLEN CARPET; FRENCH (SAVONNERIE), CA. 1800

A basket of fruit, within a circle of roses, rests on a pair of giant acanthus leaves whose spiral ends also support a pair of flaming torches. The border is of palmettes and small flowers.

340 x 245 cm. (11 ft. 2 in. x 8 ft.) Österreichisches Museum für angewandte Kunst, Vienna.

110

110. KNOTTED WOOLEN CARPET; FRENCH (SAVONNERIE), CA. 1830

The exuberant Baroque design recalls a stucco ceiling. Here the decorative elements of the eighteenth century live on, sometimes in exaggerated form.

875 x 640 cm. (28 ft. 8 in. x 21 ft.) Ghiordes or Turkish knot, approx. 30 knots per sq. in. Österreichisches Museum für angewandt Kunst, Vienna.

111. WOVEN CARPET, WOOL; (FRENCH) (AUBUSSON), FIRST HALF 18TH CENTURY

In the field are three large medallions of flared outline, filled with flowers. There is an interlacement border.

Österreichisches Museum für angewandte Kunst, Vienna.

111

NINETEENTH
CENTURY CARPETS

112

ANATOLIA (Asia Minor)

112. KNOTTED WOOLEN CARPET; HEREKE, 19TH CENTURY

The products of the Turkish Court manufacture display both traditional Eastern and European designs. In this example, the influence of Savonnerie carpets is obvious.

396 x 360 cm. (13 ft. x 11 ft. 9 in.) House of Perez (London) Ltd.

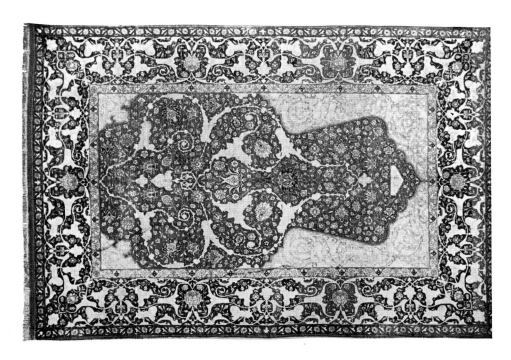

113

114

113. SILK PRAYER RUG; HEREKE, 19TH CENTURY

Mihrab and border are dominated by arabesques and scrolling stems of an almost calligraphic quality; the entire rug is strewn with small flowers—a very typical Court product. Warp and weft are cotton; pile is very short.

183 x 122 cm. (6 ft. x 4 ft.) House of Perez (London) Ltd.

114. WOOLEN PRAYER RUG; GHIORDES, 18TH CENTURY

The mihrab has a very steep gable and an inner border of carnations; rows of carnations appear in the spandrels. In the cross panels are large palmettes, smaller flowers, and S-forms. The principal border stripe also contains carnations (in groups of four) as well as flowering branches. The design here is one of the many types of decoration found in Ghiordes rugs. Warp and weft are wool or cotton. The pile is very short, the colors being chiefly red, blue, yellow, and white.

162 x 129 cm. (5 ft. 4 in. x 4 ft. 3 in.) House of Perez (London) Ltd.

115

188

116

115. WOOLEN PRAYER RUG; KULA, 19TH CENTURY

In the mihrab, within an inner border of clover leaves, are two rows of a small landscape motif of houses and cypresses (supposedly resembling a tomb); above the gable are small, closely grouped stylized flowers. The cross panels are filled with large rosettes; the multiple border, with rows of flowering branches. This is easily identified as an example of the so-called cemetery carpet (Mazarlek), because of the motif in the mihrab. Warp and weft are wool; the pile short to medium in length. Colors are red, brownish-yellow, blue, some green, dark brown, and white.
138 x 124 cm. (4 ft. 6 in. x 4 ft. 1 in.) O. Bernheimer, Munich.

116. WOOLEN PRAYER RUG; LADIK, 19TH CENTURY

The gable is crow-stepped and ornamented with finials. The cross panels above and below the mihrab are filled with a tulip and zig-zag pattern which, like the rosettes alternating with diagonal stylized flowers in the main border, is a typical Ladik motif. In the guard stripes are drawn-out, wavy scrolls. Warp and weft are wool, the weft being mostly red. The pile is of medium length. Colors are red, blue, some green, yellow, and brown.
190 x 112 cm. (6 ft. 3 in. x 3 ft. 8 in.) House of Perez (London) Ltd.

117. WOOLEN PRAYER RUG; MUDJUR, 19TH CENTURY

The mihrab has a steep crow-stepped gable outlined in several colors. The spandrels contain two ewers and are bordered by a zig-zag. The cross panel above is filled with stiff flowers. There is a characteristic lozenge border, an inner guard stripe of smaller lozenges, and an outer one of rosettes. Warp and weft are wool. The weft in this type of rug is usually red or brown. The pile is of medium length. Colors are red, yellow, blue, green, and pink.
185 x 129 cm. (6 ft. 1 in. x 4 ft. 3 in.) House of Perez (London) Ltd.

118. KNOTTED WOOLEN RUG; KIRSHEHIR, 19TH CENTURY

The gable of the mihrab is outlined in many colors. There is a carnation border within the mihrab and also in the inner field. In the cross panel are cloud bands and rosettes, and in the border are flowering branches. Warp and weft are wool; the pile is of medium length. The colors are similar to those in the Mujur rug (*Ill. 117*).
135 x 108 cm. (4 ft. 5 in. x 3 ft. 6 in.) Private collection, Vienna.

117

118

119

120

119. KNOTTED WOOLEN RUG; MAKRI (RHODES), 19TH CENTURY

The divided field contains a variety of geometric motifs. In the border are lozenges and stylized rosettes. Warp and weft are wool (the weft being red), and the pile is long. Red, blue, yellow, green, and white are the colors.

185 x 108 cm. (6 ft. 1 in. x 3 ft. 6 in.)

120. WOOLEN PRAYER RUG; MILAS, 19TH CENTURY

The upper portion of the mihrab contracts to such an extent that the gable appears almost a rhombus. There is an inner border of small leaves, a field strewn with flowers, and above the mihrab the spandrels contain large stylized carnations on a light ground. The border of medallions with rosettes and S-hooks is enclosed by tripartite guard stripes of wave bands and rows of rosettes. Warp and weft are wool. The weft in this type of rug is usually blue or red; pile is of medium length. Colors include red, some blue, yellow, and white.

142 x 104 cm. (4 ft. 8 in. x 3 ft. 5 in.) House of Perez (London) Ltd.

121

121. WOOLEN PRAYER RUG; ANATOLIAN, 19TH CENTURY

The mihrab has an inner border of flowers; the spandrels are filled with carnations. In the cross panels are large flowers (above) and a zigzag frieze (below). A diaper border with tripartite guard stripes of flowers, wavy scrolls, and S-forms encloses the mihrab. Warp and weft are wool. The weft is red. The pile is of medium length—in red, blue, green, brown, and white.
168 x 119 cm. (5 ft. 6 in. x 3 ft. 11 in.) House of Perez (London) Ltd.

122. KNOTTED WOOLEN RUG; TUZLA, 19TH CENTURY

In the mihrab, spandrel, and cross panel are stylized flowers on long stems, all within a geometric border. The octagon with the star-shaped flower arrangement is a characteristic feature. Warp and weft are wool. Colors are red, blue, green, and ivory.
145 x 120 cm. (4 ft. 9 in. x 3 ft. 11 in.) Private collection, Vienna.

122

123

124

125

123. KNOTTED WOOLEN RUG; YURUK, 19TH CENTURY

Lozenges and triangles edged with hooks appear throughout. In the principal border stripe are small lozenges with hooks; guard stripes are of reciprocal gadroons. The pile is long; the warp and weft, wool. Colors include brown, red, blue, some yellow, green, and white.

210 x 90 cm. (6 ft. 11 in. x 2 ft. 11 in.)

124. KNOTTED WOOLEN RUG; BERGAMA, CA. 1800

Within the hexagonal medallion are stylized carnations and rosettes; in the spandrels, rosettes and saw-edged leaves. The border is of palmettes and hooked lozenges. Warp and (red) weft are wool. The pile in this type of rug can be medium length or long. Colors are red, blue, some yellow, white, and green.

132 x 114 cm. (4 ft. 4 in. x 3 ft. 9 in.) House of Perez (London) Ltd.

125. KNOTTED WOOLEN RUG; BERGAMA, 19TH CENTURY

This interesting rug shows a variation of the medallion motif. Hook forms of every kind cover field and border.

177 x 147 cm. (5 ft. 10 in. x 4 ft. 10 in.) O. Bernheimer, Munich.

126

127

PERSIA

126. KNOTTED WOOLEN CARPET; TABRIZ, 19TH CENTURY

A large medallion enclosing several smaller ones occupies almost the entire field; the remainder is covered by *herati* designs in many colors. In the multiple border are various scroll motifs. Warp and weft are wool; the pile is very short. Main colors are red, blue, and ivory; the knot is Ghiordes.

630 x 404 cm. (20 ft. 8 in. x 13 ft. 3 in.) House of Perez (London) Ltd.

127. KNOTTED WOOLEN CARPET; KASHAN, 19TH CENTURY

A large medallion encloses a pendant medallion; quarter medallions appear at the corners. The whole field is covered by a profusion of flowers, some of them naturalistic. The wide border of several stripes is formed by round medallions, flowering scrolls, etc. Warp and (blue) weft are cotton; the pile is very short and soft. The Sehna or Persian knot is used. Dark blue, red, ivory, yellowish brown, light blue, and green are the colors.

315 x 221 cm. (10 ft. 4 in. x 7 ft. 3 in.) House of Perez (London) Ltd.

128

200

129

128. KNOTTED WOOLEN CARPET; MESHED, 19TH CENTURY

A large medallion encloses a smaller, star-shaped one. Field and border stripes are covered by flowering scrolls. Warp and weft are wool; the pile of medium length. The Sehna knot is usually employed in this type of carpet. Colors are red, pink, blue, white, some yellow, and green.

O. Bernheimer, Munich.

129. KNOTTED WOOLEN CARPET; ISFAHAN, 19TH CENTURY

This design is completely dominated by the influence of carpets of the Classic period. Flowering scrolls, cloud bands, and arabesques are everywhere. The border contains giant flower-heads and birds amid spiral scrolls. Warp and weft in this type of carpet are usually wool. The pile is short to medium length. Ghiordes or Turkish knot; red, blue, green, and yellow are the colors.

405 x 295 cm. (13 ft. 3 in. x 9 ft. 8 in.) O. Bernheimer, Munich.

**130. KNOTTED WOOLEN CARPET; KERMAN,
19TH CENTURY**

This prayer carpet has an elaborate mihrab filled with cypresses, vases, and flowering branches. In the border are medallions with peacocks, cloud bands, and flowers. Warp and weft in this type of carpet are usually cotton; pile is short and silky. Sehna or Persian knot. Colors: ivory, light brown, yellow, pink, and blue. The Kerman carpets of the nineteenth century are often called Laver Kermans, a distortion of the name Ravar Kerman, the principal center of production. The trade therefore prefers simply the designation Kerman.

345 x 276 cm. (11 ft. 4 in. x 9 ft. 1 in.) House of Perez (London) Ltd.

131

131. KNOTTED WOOLEN CARPET; HEREZ, 19TH CENTURY

The designs of Herez and Gorevan carpets are based on Classic motifs: medallion schemes, joined corner pieces, flowering scrolls in the rest of the field, scrolls and arabesques in the border. But the flowing lines of the carpets of Tabriz have become stiff and angular. Warp and weft are cotton. Pile is medium length. Ghiordes or Turkish knot; colors: ivory, light blue, reddish-brown, yellow, and green.

410 x 280 cm. (13 ft. 6 in. x 9 ft. 2 in.) O. Bernheimer, Munich.

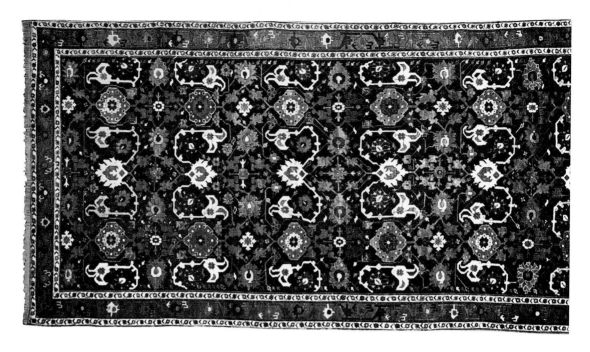

132

133

204

132. KNOTTED WOOLEN CARPET; KARADAGH, 19TH CENTURY

The field is covered in an all-over pattern of large flower-heads, rosettes, and arabesques reminiscent of Caucasian rugs. The border contains angular scrolls. Warp and weft wool; pile medium length; Ghiordes or Turkish knot. The colors are blue, red, yellow, and white.

409 x 213 cm. (13 ft. 5 in. x 7 ft.) House of Perez (London) Ltd.

133. KNOTTED WOOLEN CARPET; FERAGHAN, 19TH CENTURY

The field is closely covered with a *herati* pattern; in the border are scrolls with large palmette flowers. The *herati* pattern and *herati* border, which originated in eastern Persia, are revived most successfully in the carpets of the Feraghan region. Warp and weft are wool. The pile is short, and usually the Sehna knot is used. Red and dark blue with yellow, light blue, green, and white are the colors.

295 x 150 cm. (9 ft. 8 in. x 4 ft. 11 in.) House of Perez (London) Ltd.

134. KNOTTED WOOLEN RUG; SARABEND, 19TH CENTURY

The field in this type of rug is almost invariably filled with the Sarabend cone or *boteh* pattern, arranged so that the stems in adjoining rows turn in opposite directions. In the spandrels are stylized flowers; the principal border stripe contains a wavy scroll design. Warp and weft are cotton. The weft in this type of rug can be red or blue. Pile, short to medium length; Sehna or Persian knot. Colors are red or blue with ivory, yellow, and green.

180 x 113 cm. (5 ft. 11 in. x 3 ft. 8 in.) In the possession of a Viennese dealer.

135. KNOTTED WOOLEN RUG; HAMADAN, 19TH CENTURY

The medallion in this example has become a hexagon enclosing a star-shaped arrangement of leaves and flowers. In the rest of the field are stiff stems and a repetition of the hexagon motif (only part shown). Two wide border stripes—flowering scrolls and reciprocal trefoils—are enclosed within a broad outer border of plain camel's hair. Warp and weft are mostly cotton; pile is usually short. Ghiordes or Turkish knot is employed. Colors are natural camel, red, and blue.

Victoria and Albert Museum, London.

134

135

136

137

136. KNOTTED WOOLEN RUG; TAFRISH
(HAMADAN REGION), CA. 1900

Centered on the light ground is a medallion of stiff flowers; above
and below is an arrangement of six vases packed with flowers. These
vases are repeated in the border. This pattern is called Zil-i-Soltan,
after a Quajar prince who was Governor of Isfahan in 1890.
208 x 117 cm. (6 ft. 10 in. x 3 ft. 10 in.) House of Perez (London) Ltd.

137. KNOTTED WOOLEN RUG; JOSHAGAN,
19TH CENTURY

Most of the field is taken up by a medallion with large, vigorously
outlined flowers and leaves. The two principal border stripes (of
equal width and similar design) contain hyacinths and rosettes.
Warp and weft in this type of rug can be wool or cotton. Pile is
short to medium length. Ghiordes or Turkish knot is used. Red,
blue, some yellow, green, brown, and ivory are the colors.
208 x 150 cm. (6 ft. 10 in. x 4 ft. 11 in.) House of Perez (London) Ltd.

138

138. KNOTTED WOOLEN CARPET; SAROUK, 19TH CENTURY

Giant flower-heads, rosettes, and flowering branches are set within sturdy arabesques. The principal border contains a scrolling stem with giant flower-heads; wavy scrolls appear in the guard stripe. Warp and weft are cotton, the weft being blue. Pile is short and velvety. Sehna or Persian knot. Colors are dark blue, red with green, olive, and ivory.
298 x 217 cm. (9 ft. 9 in. x 7 ft. 1 in.) O. Bernheimer, Munich.

139. KNOTTED WOOLEN RUG; SEHNA (SINNEH), 19TH CENTURY

The entire field is covered with the *herati* pattern. The border is of large flower-heads and lanceolate leaves. Warp and weft are cotton. Pile is very short. Both the Sehna and Ghiordes knot are used in this type of rug. Colors are dark blue, red, ivory, some green, light blue, and yellow.
208 x 147 cm. (6 ft. 10 in. x 4 ft. 10 in.) House of Perez (London) Ltd.

139

140. KNOTTED WOOLEN CARPET; BIJAR, 19TH CENTURY

The elongated medallion with the anchor pendants and the corner pieces reminiscent of curtains are both covered with the *herati* pattern; the rest of the field is plain. The border contains scrolls and palmettes. Warp and weft are wool. Pile is medium length. Ghiordes or Turkish knot; red, blue, ivory, green, yellow, and brown are the colors.
560 x 350 cm. (18 ft. 4 in. x 11 ft. 6 in.) O. Bernheimer, Munich.

141. KNOTTED WOOLEN CARPET; SULTANABAD, 19TH CENTURY

Large rosettes are centered within lozenges formed by saw-edged leaves; flowering scrolls form the border. Warp and weft are cotton; pile is medium length. Both the Ghiordes or Turkish and the Sehna or Persian knot are used in this type of carpet. Colors are red, blue, ivory, green, and brown.
473 x 180 cm. (15 ft. 6 in. x 5 ft. 11 in.)

142. KNOTTED WOOLEN RUG; SAUJBULAGH, 19TH CENTURY

The field is filled with the *mina khani* pattern and small horses; in the three stripes of the border are flowering scrolls. The general impression of these nomad rugs is one of dark colors. Warp and weft wool; pile medium length; Ghiordes or Turkish knot. The colors include dark red and blue, as well as brown, green, yellow, and ivory.

140

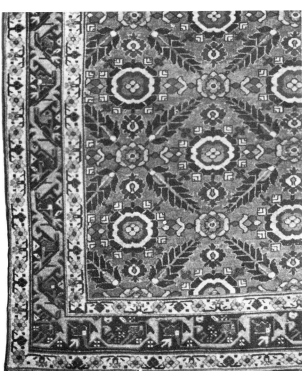

141

142

213

143

214

144

143. KNOTTED WOOLEN RUG; MOSUL, 19TH CENTURY

A network of thin lines divides the field into lozenges, which are
filled with rosettes. The border, too, contains rosettes and also stiff
stems. Warp and weft wool; pile medium length; Ghiordes or Turkish knot. Yellow, brownish-red, some blue, green, and white are the
colors.

188 x 155 cm. (6 ft. 2 in. x 5 ft. 1 in.)

144. KNOTTED WOOLEN RUG; KURDISTAN, 19TH CENTURY

The field here is divided into three rectangles, each containing three
stylized flowers outlined with hooks. The principal border stripe
contains stylized stars; the guard stripes, rosettes and S-forms. Kurdistan rugs are typical nomad products, having an almost infinite
variety of designs. Warp and weft, wool. Pile, medium length.
Ghiordes or Turkish knot. Colors are red, blue, yellow, green, and
white.

236 x 122 cm. (7 ft. 9 in. x 4 ft.) House of Perez (London) Ltd.

145

146

145. KNOTTED WOOLEN RUG; KHURASAN, 19TH CENTURY

The entire field is covered with the *boteh* pattern, set within symmetric flowering scrolls. In the border are small cypresses and flowering scrolls. Warp and weft are cotton; pile is silky and of medium length. Sehna knot. Pink, blue, ivory, yellow, and green.
218 x 132 cm. (7 ft. 2 in. x 4 ft. 4 in.) House of Perez (London) Ltd.

146. KNOTTED WOOLEN CARPET; KAIN (QAIN), 19TH CENTURY

A close *mina khani* pattern covers the field. The principal border stripe contains flowering tendrils with large rosettes. Warp and weft cotton; pile medium length; Sehna or Persian knot. Pink, blue, ivory, yellow, and green.
390 x 212 cm. (12 ft. 9 in. x 6 ft. 11 in.)

147. KNOTTED WOOLEN RUG; SHIRAZ, 19TH CENTURY

A medallion of angular outline is echoed in similar corner pieces scattered with small flowers; the space between is filled with large *boteh* motifs. Barber pole motif and scrolling stems are used in the border stripes.

200 x 135 cm. (6 ft. 7 in. x 4 ft. 5 in.)

148. KNOTTED WOOLEN CARPET; SHIRAZ, 19TH CENTURY

Three hexagonal pole medallions are filled with hooks and dots. In the rest of the field is a variety of stars, lozenges, octagons, and other geometric or highly stylized forms. The multiple border contains rosette and barber pole stripes. Warp and weft are wool, and the pile is short to medium in length. Both the Ghiordes and Sehna knot are used in this type of rug. Colors are blue, red, ivory, yellow, and green.

300 x 180 cm. (9 ft. 10 in. x 5 ft. 11 in.) O. Bernheimer, Munich.

148

149

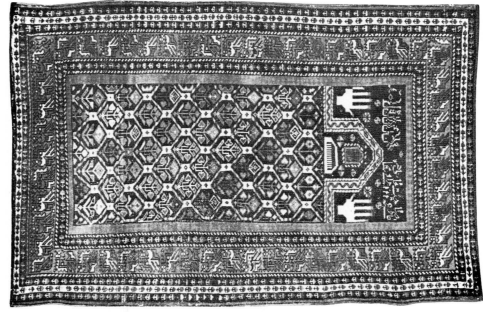

150

CAUCASUS

149. KNOTTED WOOLEN RUG; DAGHESTAN, 19TH CENTURY

The field is divided into small-patterned, diagonal bands. In the main border stripe are large rosettes. Warp and weft wool. Pile short. Ghiordes or Turkish knot. Colors: blue, red, ivory, some green, and yellow.

126 x 96 cm. (4 ft. 2 in. x 3 ft. 2 in.)

150. WOOLEN PRAYER RUG; DAGHESTAN, 19TH CENTURY

The field of the mihrab is divided into small hexagons, each enclosing a flowering branch. In the border stripes are stylized flowering branches and rosettes.

135 x 89 cm. (4 ft. 5 in. x 2 ft. 11 in.) House of Perez (London) Ltd.

151

151. KNOTTED WOOLEN CARPET; DERBENT, 19TH CENTURY

Between rows of rosettes linked by stiff stems are the split-leaf arabesques already characteristic of early Caucasian rugs. Border stripes contain wavy scrolls. Warp and weft in this type of rug can be wool or cotton. Pile is medium length. Ghiordes or Turkish knot. Red, ivory, some green, yellow, and brown.
360 x 180 cm. (11 ft. 10 in. x 5 ft. 11 in.) O. Bernheimer, Munich.

152

152. KNOTTED WOOLEN RUG; LEZGHIAN, 19TH CENTURY

Three joined, star-shaped medallions run along the central axis. In the rest of the field are various geometric designs. There is a characteristic Caucasian border of diagonal saw-edged leaves and small tulips. Warp and weft wool. Pile medium length. Ghiordes or Turkish knot. Colors are blue, yellow, red, brown, and ivory.
298 x 130 cm. (9 ft. 9 in. x 4 ft. 3 in.) From a private collection in Graz, Austria.

153

154

224

153. KNOTTED WOOLEN RUG; KUBA, 19TH CENTURY

Six closely-grouped, hexagonal medallions filled with lozenges and rosettes cover the center of the field; the rest of the field contains various characteristically Caucasian, geometric forms. Angular rosettes between saw-edged leaves make up the main border stripe.
259 x 102 cm. (8 ft. 6 in. x 3 ft. 4 in.) House of Perez (London) Ltd.

154. KNOTTED WOOLEN RUG; KABISTAN, 19TH CENTURY

The leaf ends of the arabesques form a rectangular pattern which dominates the field and makes the rosettes and stars appear of secondary importance. The border is Kufic. Warp and weft wool; pile medium length; Ghiordes or Turkish knot. Colors are blue, some red, ivory, green, and brown.
389 x 114 cm. (12 ft. 9 in. x 3 ft. 9 in.) House of Perez (London) Ltd.

155. KNOTTED WOOLEN RUG; SHIRVAN, 19TH CENTURY

Almost the entire field is occupied by a long medallion of angular outline, enclosing stars and octagons. In the two principal border stripes appears one of the earliest Caucasian motifs, diagonal saw-edged leaves with tulips on stiff stems. Warp and weft wool. Pile short to medium length. Ghiordes or Turkish knot. Blue, red, and ivory.
190 x 137 cm. (6 ft. 3 in. x 4 ft. 6 in.) House of Perez (London) Ltd.

155

156

156. KNOTTED WOOLEN RUG; CHICHI, 19TH CENTURY

The field is packed with rows of octagons and hooked stars. The main border stripe of rosettes and diagonal leaves is characteristically Chichi. Warp and weft wool. Pile short or medium length. Ghiordes or Turkish knot. Ivory, blue, red, some green, and brown.
185 x 122 cm. (6 ft. 1 in. x 4 ft.) House of Perez (London) Ltd.

157. KNOTTED WOOLEN RUG; SEICHUR, 19TH CENTURY

Star-shaped medallions, alternating with a design of flowering branches, fill the field. In the outer border stripe is a variation of the running dog pattern. Warp and weft in this type of rug are usually wool. Pile short to medium length. Ghiordes or Turkish knot. Colors are ivory, red, yellow, green, and blue.
170 x 100 cm. (5 ft. 6 in. x 3 ft. 3 in.)

157

158. KNOTTED WOOLEN CARPET; BAKU, 19TH CENTURY

Three medallions enclose smaller ones; medallion quarters appear at the corners. The rest of the field contains large-patterned *boteh* forms within adjoining hexagons. The border stripes are of rosettes and diagonal bands. Warp and weft in this type of rug are usually wool. Piles is short. Ghiordes or Turkish knot. Brown, blue, yellow, and black are the colors.

363 x 152 cm. (11 ft. 11 in. x 5 ft.) House of Perez (London) Ltd.

159. WOVEN WOOLEN CARPET; SOUMAK, 19TH CENTURY

Three large, joined rectangles are filled with geometric designs. In the border stripes are rows of octagons, stars, and plaitwork bands; in the outer guard stripe is the characteristic Soumak version of the running dog pattern. Warp and weft wool. Colors: red, blue, brown, yellow, and white.

280 x 180 cm. (9 ft. 2 in. x 5 ft. 11 in.) O. Bernheimer, Munich.

**160. KNOTTED WOOLEN RUG; SHEMAKHA,
19TH CENTURY**

The field is divided into a series of rectangles enclosing medallions filled with flowering branches and outlined with rays. In the spandrels are giant flower-heads. Kufic designs and rosette make up the border stripes. These rugs used to be known in the trade as Royal Daghestans. Warp and weft wool. Pile medium length. Ghiordes or Turkish knot. Blue, red, and brown.
O. Bernheimer, Munich.

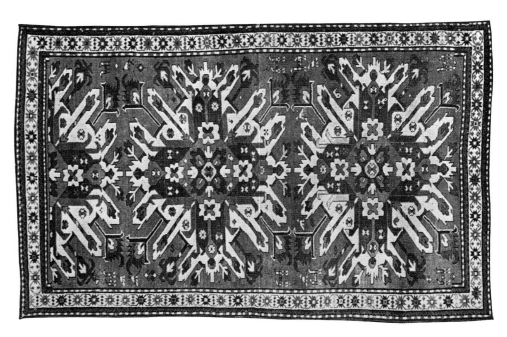

161

162

232

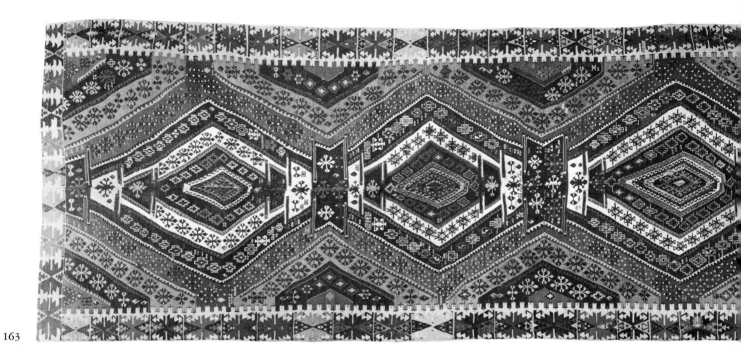

163

161. KNOTTED WOOLEN RUG; KAZAK, 19TH CENTURY

The sunburst medallions, with flowers on stiff stems between the bandlike rays, enclose rosettes. The main border stripe is of rosettes linked by angular scrolls. Rugs of this design are also known as Eagle Kazaks. Warp and weft wool. Pile medium length. Ghiordes or Turkish knot. Colors are red, brown, yellow, blue, and white.
223 x 145 cm. (7 ft. 4 in. x 4 ft. 9 in.) House of Perez (London) Ltd.

162. KNOTTED WOOLEN RUG; KAZAK, 19TH CENTURY

A large pendant medallion extends into two smaller ones; all contain S-forms, stars, and hooks. The border is of stylized carnations with lanceolate leaves—one of the many Kazak designs.
220 x 160 cm. (7 ft. 3 in. x 5 ft. 3 in.) O. Bernheimer, Munich.

163. WOVEN WOOLEN CARPET (KILIM); KARABAGH, 19TH CENTURY

Practically the entire field is taken up by joined, lozenge-shaped medallions formed by bands filled with geometric motifs. In the border are rosettes with saw-edged outlines and hooks. Warp and weft wool. Pile short or medium length. Ghiordes or Turkish knot. Red, blue, yellow, and white.
373 x 154 cm. (12 ft. 3 in. x 5 ft. 1 in.) O. Bernheimer, Munich.

164

164. KNOTTED WOOLEN CARPET; SHUSHA, 19TH CENTURY

In an otherwise almost bare field appears a succession of anchor-shaped hexagonal medallions filled with small geometric designs. Border stripes contain flowers, scrolling stems, and diagonal leaves. Warp and weft wool. Pile medium length. Ghiordes or Turkish knot. Colors: red, blue, white, some yellow, brown, and black.
O. Bernheimer, Munich.

165. KNOTTED WOOLEN RUG; GENDJEH, 19TH CENTURY

A large octagonal medallion is filled with octagons and stars; large stars also appear in the main border stripe. Warp and weft wool. Pile medium length. Ghiordes or Turkish knot. Colors are blue, red, white, some green, yellow, and brown.
148 x 114 cm. (4 ft. 10 in. x 3 ft. 9 in.) O. Bernheimer, Munich.

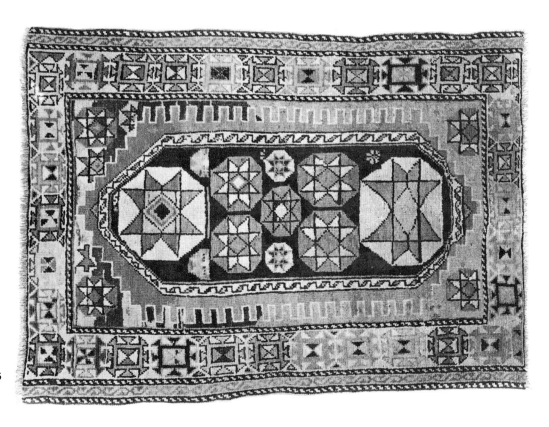

165

166

236

167

166. WOVEN WOOLEN RUG; VERNEH, 19TH CENTURY

The ground is divided into rectangles and squares enclosing stylized
animals. Woven carpets (see *Ill. 163*) are often made in sections and
joined. Colors: red, ivory, and yellow.
150 x 120 cm. (4 ft. 11 in. x 3 ft. 11 in.)

167. WOVEN WOOLEN CARPET; SILEH,
18TH/19TH CENTURY

A design of large, dark and light Z-forms, some supported by small
trees, covers the entire field. In between, an hourglass-shaped motif
is repeated. The Z-pattern possibly represents highly stylized and
simplified dragons. Colors are red, ivory, and yellow.
270 x 190 cm. (8 ft. 10 in. x 6 ft. 3 in.) Österreichisches Museum für angewandte Kunst.

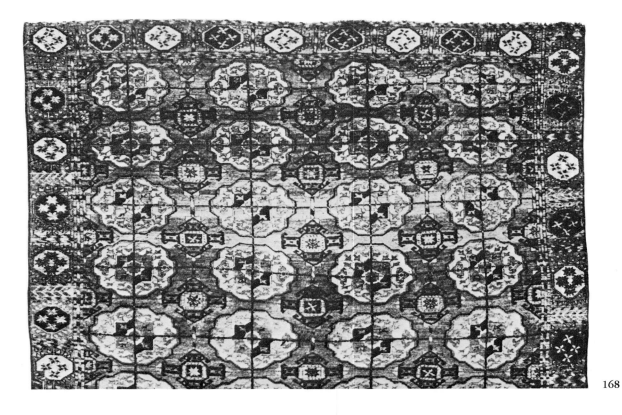

168

169

238

TURKESTAN

Even the highly tradition-bound Turkoman rugs had no completely rigid tribal patterns. There may have been some connection between the geometric designs of Western Turkestan and the 15th- and 16th-century rugs of Asia Minor. In Eastern Turkestan, Chinese influence predominated.

168. KNOTTED WOOLEN RUG; TEKKE-TURKOMAN, 19TH CENTURY

At the intersecting points of a network of thin lines appear the characteristic quartered Turkoman polygons (*guls*). Between these are smaller elongated polygons, all within a polygon border. Warp and weft wool. Pile short. Sehna or Persian knot. Colors: dark red or maroon, shades of plum, brown, some dark blue and ivory.

169. KNOTTED WOOLEN RUG; SALOR-TURKOMAN, 19TH CENTURY

Rows of octagons are outlined by zigzag forms and filled with geometric designs. Warp and weft are wool; the pile is short. Sehna or Persian knot. Colors: dark red, some blue, orange, and ivory.

170

171

170. KNOTTED WOOLEN RUG; PENDEH-TURKOMAN, 19TH CENTURY

Rows of octagons alternate with rows of star-shaped medallions. In the border are rosettes within octagons; the end borders are filled with designs of zigzag stripes. Warp and weft are wool. The pile in this type of rug is short to medium length. Sehna or Persian knot. Colors: dark red, brown, some dark blue, and ivory.

99 x 97 cm. (3 ft. 3 in. x 3 ft. 2 in.) House of Perez (London) Ltd.

171. KNOTTED WOOLEN RUG; KHIVA-TURKOMAN, 19TH CENTURY

A Khatchli with the field divided diagonally by a white cross formed of lozenges and horizontally by a series of lines, with darker lozenges between the arms of the cross. The border contains star-shaped rosettes. Warp and weft are wool; pile is medium length. Both the Sehna and the Ghiordes knot are used in this type of rug. Colors are dark red, brown, some dark blue, and ivory.

150 x 128 cm. (4 ft. 11 in. x 4 ft. 2 in.)

240

172. KNOTTED WOOLEN CARPET; BESHIR-TURKOMAN, 19TH CENTURY

The entire field is covered by a lattice design of lozenges and hexagons. Warp and weft are wool. Pile is medium length. Sehna or Persian knot. Dark red and brown, some blue, yellow, and white are the colors.

345 x 145 cm. (11 ft. 4 in. x 4 ft. 9 in.) O. Bernheimer, Munich.

173. KNOTTED WOOLEN RUG; BESHIR-TURKOMAN, 19TH CENTURY

A prayer rug. Within the white field of the mihrab are rows of small flowers and a panel with broad, wavy stems on a red ground. Beshirs, in contrast to other Turkoman rugs, often contain stylized flowers in the design.

127 x 90 cm. (4 ft. 2 in. x 2 ft. 11 in.) O. Bernheimer, Munich.

174

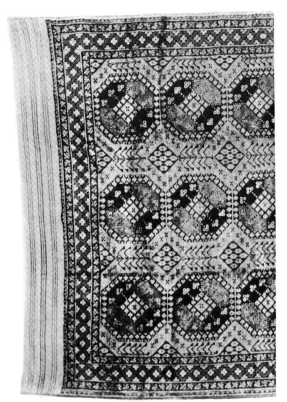

175

176

177

174. KNOTTED WOOLEN CARPET; BESHIR-TURKOMAN, 19TH CENTURY

Apart from a small medallion, the entire field is covered by broad cloud bands, hooks, and dots. A narrow scrolling stem forms the border.

320 x 150 cm. (10 ft. 6 in. x 4 ft. 11 in.)

175. KNOTTED WOOLEN CARPET; AFGHAN, 19TH CENTURY

The field is divided into a network of quartered octagons, filled with a design of stylized leaves. In the lozenge-shaped spaces formed by adjoining octagons are stylized leaves on stiff stems. The border is lattice. Warp and weft are wool; pile, medium length. The Sehna or Persian knot is usually used. Dark red, brown, some blue, green, yellow, and white.

176. KNOTTED WOOLEN RUG; BALUCHISTAN, 19TH CENTURY

Alternating rows of octagons, the sides decorated with hooks, cover the field. The border is of stylized flowers on stiff stems and reciprocal gadroons.

240 x 150 cm. (7 ft. 10 in. x 4 ft. 11 in.)

177. KNOTTED WOOLEN RUG; YOMUD-TURKOMAN, 19TH CENTURY

Alternating rows of small, elongated octagons, not unlike pendant medallions, fill the field. In the characteristic border are large stylized flowers. Warp and weft wool. Pile medium length. Usually Sehna or Persian knot. Colors: dark red, brown, some blue, green, and white.

178

178. KNOTTED WOOLEN RUG; YOMUD-TURKOMAN, 19TH CENTURY

A Khatchli with the red field divided by a white cross (formed of rosettes) into four rectangles; within the latter is a network of lines. End borders contain stylized giant flower-heads and a characteristic zigzag motif.

168 x 156 cm. (5 ft. 6 in. x 5 ft. 1 in.) O. Bernheimer, Munich.

179. KNOTTED SILK CARPET (FRAGMENT); SAMARKAND, CA. 1800

On the red ground are rosettes of various colors; the principal border stripes contain a meander design and a Chinese motif representing sea waves breaking over rocks. Warp and weft cotton. Pile is medium length. Sehna or Persian knot. Colors are red, blue, and yellow.

235 x 118 cm. (7 ft. 8 in. x 3 ft. 10 in.) O. Bernheimer, Munich.

179

180

181

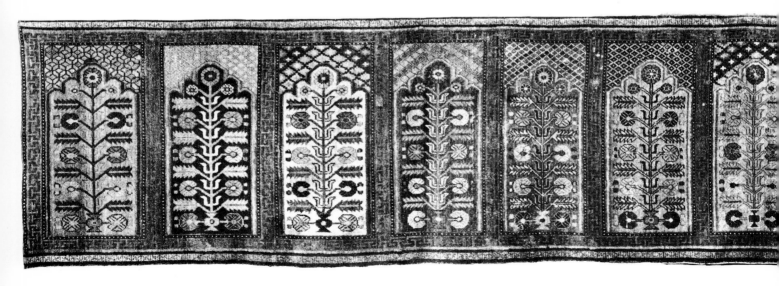

182

180. KNOTTED WOOLEN RUG; KASHGAR, 19TH CENTURY

In the field and the wide main border stripe are large stylized flowers. Guard stripes display a meander design. Warp and weft cotton. Pile medium length. Dark blue and dark red; often also lighter shades.

270 x 130 cm. (8 ft. 10 in. x 4 ft. 3 in.) O. Bernheimer, Munich.

181. FAMILY PRAYER RUG (WOOL); SAMARKAND, 19TH CENTURY

In the mihrabs are small vases with large stylized flowers and leaves on stiff stems. The border has a meander design.

90 x 305 cm. (2 ft. 11 in. x 10 ft.) O. Bernheimer, Munich.

182. KNOTTED WOOLEN RUG; KHOTAN, 19TH CENTURY

The field contains three round, star-filled medallions set among stiff stems. The border is a Chinese motif of sea waves breaking over rocks. Warp and weft are wool; pile, medium length. Sehna or Persian knot. Colors are red, blue, and yellow.

270 x 130 cm. (8 ft. 10 in. x 4 ft. 3 in.) O. Bernheimer, Munich.

183

PERSIA

In the twentieth century, the design of the Persian carpet is governed by two considerations: the requirements of a Western clientele and the revival of the great tradition of the Safavid dynasty.

183. KNOTTED WOOLEN CARPET; RAVAR, CA. 1914

The design contains Indian as well as Persian elements, particularly in the naturalistic rendering of trees. The border of large flower-heads alternating with rosettes is in the traditional Persian taste.

184. KNOTTED WOOLEN CARPET; SAROUK, CA. 1935

The field is covered with a design of large, flowering branches. Along the border, pointing inward, and in the border itself are flowers sprouting from oddly shaped panels. European influence is unmistakable.

185. KNOTTED WOOLEN CARPET; TABRIZ, CA. 1930

The arrangement of the medallions is still in the popular tradition. Between the medallions appear animals in combat, birds, and plants.

186. KNOTTED WOOLEN CARPET; TABRIZ, CA. 1935

The bizarre shape of the medallion is accentuated by the flowering scrolls. Flowering branches form the link with the corner pieces. In the border are cypresses and hyacinths.

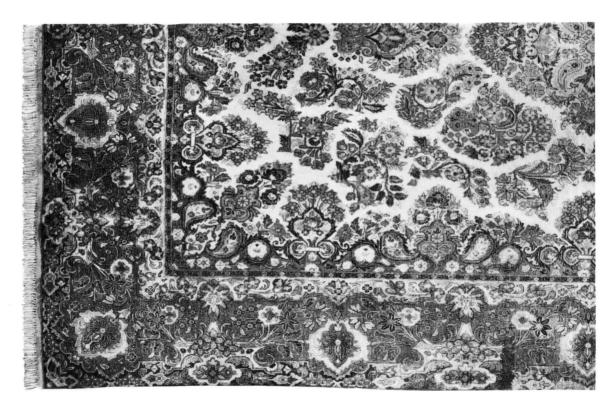

184

185

186

187

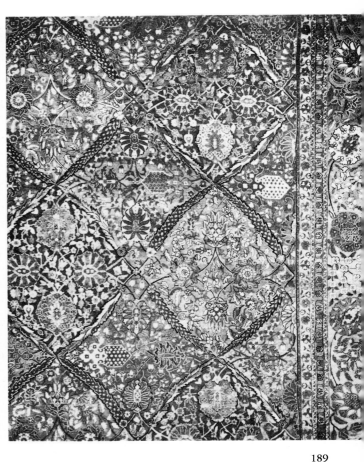

189

187. KNOTTED WOOLEN CARPET; MESHED, CA. 1935

Though the field includes many decorative elements of the great age of the Persian carpet, the composition lacks unity. The border might almost be a direct copy.

188. KNOTTED WOOLEN CARPET; MESHED, CA. 1945

A design clearly inspired by the 16th and 17th-century tiles.

189. KNOTTED WOOLEN CARPET; KERMAN, CA. 1925

The design, by Sheikh Hossein, is best described as highly derivative, both in the division of the field into lozenge-shaped compartments filled with flowers, and in the flowering-scroll border.

188

253

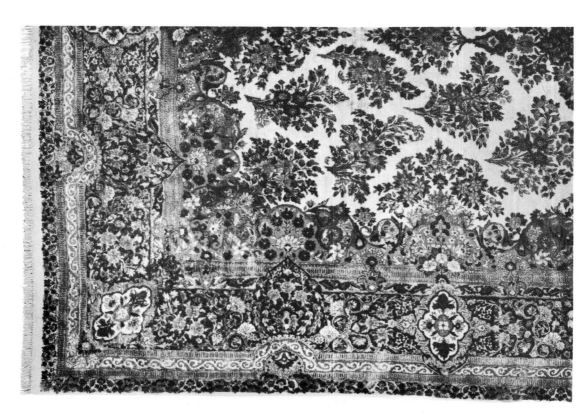

190. KNOTTED WOOLEN CARPET; KERMAN, CA. 1945

The decoration of the field—large bouquets of flowers—and the wide broken border suggest a European design. These patterns, introduced into Arak (Sultanabad) in the early twenties, have more recently also been adopted in Kerman.

191. KNOTTED WOOLEN RUG; KASHAN, CA. 1910

Almost the entire field is taken up by a lozenge enclosing a medallion set amid flowering branches. In the corners, barely more than indicated, are medallion quarters. The design obviously is derived from tribal rugs.

192. KNOTTED WOOLEN RUG; KASHAN, CA. 1948

An all-over pattern of vases filled with flowers; in the border is a similar motif. This rug is another example of the mingling of Eastern and Western elements.

191

192

255

193. KNOTTED WOOLEN RUG; ISFAHAN, CA. 1925

Flowering trees and animals of every kind, clearly Indian in inspiration, cover field and border. Attempts at perspective can be noticed in places.

MAKING A CARPET,
BUYING A CARPET,
THE CARE OF CARPETS

MAKING A CARPET

To make a carpet we need, above all, a loom. The simplest type, used by nomadic tribes, consists of two poles around which the warp threads (the chain) are tied. To stretch the warp—its position in this case is horizontal—stakes or wooden plugs have to be driven into the ground (*Fig. 31*). When the tribe moves on, the loom is simply rolled up without detaching the rug, and work can be resumed later without any difficulty. Rugs obviously have to be kept fairly narrow under such conditions.

There are several kinds of upright loom. The so-called village type consists of a fixed horizontal upper beam and a lower or cloth beam, the ends of which fit into the slots of two vertical beams. It thus resembles a frame. The weavers sit on a plank resting on the bottom rungs of two ladders. As the work proceeds, the plank is raised (*Fig. 32*).

The Tabriz type of loom makes it possible to weave carpets about twice the length of the distance between the horizontal beams, which again fit into slots of the two long side (vertical) pieces, where they are kept in position with wooden pegs (*Fig. 33*). There is no need for the weaver to change his position. When a large section of the carpet is completed, the warp is simply loosened by removing the wedges, and pulled further down; the finished portion slides up behind. The wedges are replaced, and work continues.

The roller type of loom can carry carpets of any length. Both beams are movable (*Fig. 34*). A simple mechanism is used to separate the alternate warp strings into two sets or leaves, thus creating a shed through which the warp can be passed with the shuttle. The balls of colored wool for the pile are hung across the loom at a convenient height.

MATERIAL   The principal materials are sheep's wool, silk, and cotton. Sheep's wool is still used almost universally for the pile, and to a lesser degree for warp and weft. Silk is employed in particularly fine rugs and carpets, both for the pile and the warp and weft. Cotton, like silk preferred for warp and weft, occasionally appears in the pile of Anatolian rugs when a particularly brilliant white is desired. Silk threads wound with gold or silver threads are sometimes used as brocading in very precious rugs or carpets. They are invariably woven into the fabric, since their glitter shows only when they lie flat (*Ill. 38*).

COMBINATION OF MAIN   The combination of the three chief materials varies. Only the
MATERIALS   finest examples of Persian Court manufacture are made entirely of silk (up to over 800 knots per sq. in.). The Polonaise rugs of the seventeenth century have a silk pile, though warp and weft are mostly cotton (200 to 250 knots per sq. in.). In many outstanding Persian carpets of the Safavid period, warp and weft are silk, though the pile is wool (300 to 450 knots per sq. in.). Most Persian carpets, however, have a cotton warp and weft, wool being used for the pile (90 to 180 knots per sq. in.). The same is true of Indian carpets (up to over 400 knots per sq. in.). A cotton warp with woolen weft and pile is not unknown in Persia, where rugs made entirely of sheep's wool are very rarely found, though this limitation to one material is quite usual in Egyptian and Anatolian as well as the earliest

Fig. 31   Nomad horizontal loom

Fig. 32   Village-type loom

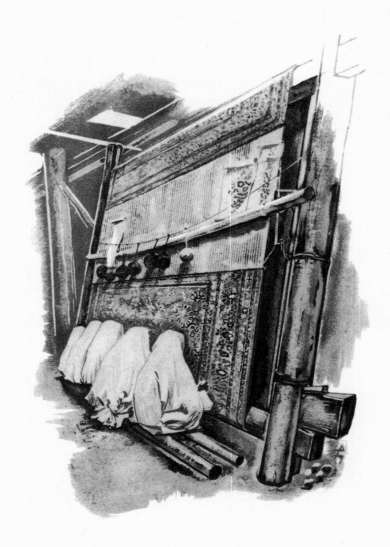

Fig. 33   Tabriz-type loom

Fig. 34   Roller-type loom

Fig. 35   A Kurdish woman spinning

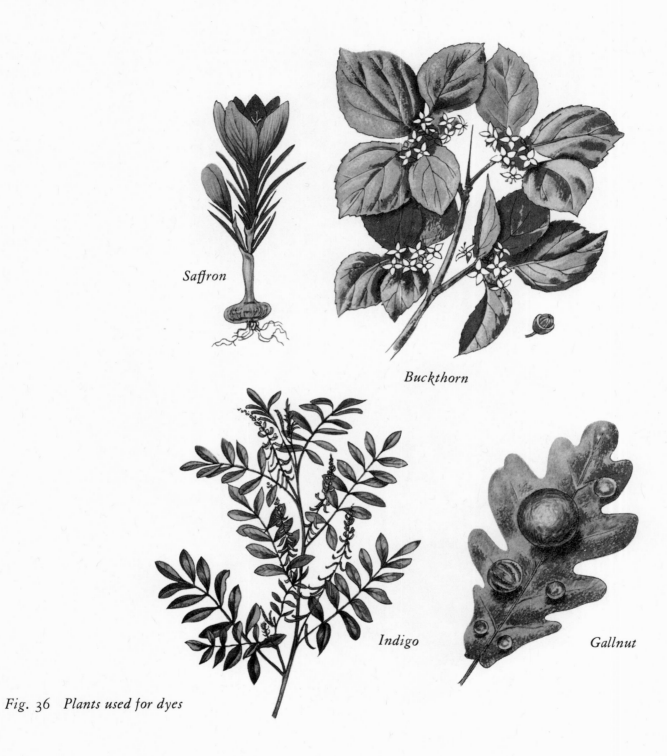

Saffron

Buckthorn

Indigo

Gallnut

Fig. 36   Plants used for dyes

Madder

Weld

Sumac

Fig. 37   Clipping the pile of the finished carpet

Caucasian examples (the so-called dragon rugs). But with the spread of Persian influence, wool quickly yields to cotton for warp and weft even in the Caucasus.

The art of dyeing is obviously of great importance. The finer the knotting, the more colors needed to achieve a well-graded design free from monotony. Vegetable dyes are still widely used (*Fig. 36*). Red is made of the madder plant, a perennial whose root, ground and dried, can be used only if the plant is at least three and not more than seven years old. Yellow is supplied by the stalks, leaves, and flowers of weld, a member of the reseda family, as well as the leaves of sumac and saffron. Green is obtained by mixing blue and yellow, or from buckthorn. The indigo plant provides blue; browns and blacks are produced from walnut shells, the bark of oak, and gallnuts. Reds are also made of insects, the cochineal and the kermes; shades of gray and black from logwood and iron oxide. But black of mineral origin affects the wool adversely, and therefore it often happens that the black or gray portions of old carpets appear much more worn than the rest. The use of natural sheep's wool is not very successful, since the black will soon fade to a dull brown. All kinds of shades can be produced by mixing.

Before dyeing can begin, the wool or silk has to be washed. Since the yarn was usually dyed in small quantities, the colors in older rugs are rarely uniform. This effect has been artificially produced in more recent examples and in machine-made carpets.

Aniline dyes were first used in the fifties of the last century. They soon enjoyed great popularity even in the East, where, temporarily, they almost replaced the ancient vegetable dyes. At the beginning of the present century, the Persian government banned the use of synthetic colors, threatening offenders with the loss of the right hand. But the ban was never completely effective because it did not extend to adjoining countries, and—not least—because chemical dyes were so much cheaper and easier to apply.

Whether the carpet has a fine or a coarse texture largely depends on the spacing and selection of the warp threads. After attaching the warp, a short web end, known in the East as "kilim" (a woven fabric), is formed by passing the weft several times across the warp threads. The first row of knots is then worked across the entire width. Traditional tribal or family designs are worked from memory, others from patterns or to instructions that are chanted or read aloud (*Figs. 42 and 43*). The pattern-forming knot is usually wound around two adjoining warp threads—in the case of the Ghiordes or Turkish knot, from above, the ends of the piece of yarn being brought forward together between the two adjoining warp threads (*Fig. 39*). In the Sehna or Persian knot the yarn encircles only alternate warp threads (*Fig. 40*). The Sehna knot can be worked from the right or the left. In recent years, the yarn has often been wound over four instead of two warp threads. This method, though saving of time and material, hardly makes for quality.

TYPES OF KNOTS

The Ghiordes knot is used in the western realms of the Oriental rug—Asia Minor (Anatolia) and the Caucasus; the Sehna knot in Persia, India, Turkestan, and China. The borderline runs, roughly, through western Persia. The nomadic Kurds use the Ghiordes; the Persian carpet workshops the Sehna. The Ghiordes is also used in the West and in mechanical production. Spanish carpets are an exception. Here, the knot is formed on one warp thread, alternating every other one in a row, and also alternating rows (*Fig. 41*). To discover the particular type of knotting used, one must take up the carpet and push the pile back with the fingers to reveal the base of a row of knots.

DIRECTION OF PILE

As the knots are being made, the yarn is firmly pulled downward. The direction of the pile, thus determined from the very start, indicates at which end the carpet was begun. Color effects, particularly in silk rugs, may vary greatly according to the direction of the pile.

When a row of knots has been completed, at least one weft thread is inserted. The weft threads are firmly pushed back with a comb to make a structure of even closeness. This process is repeated until the carpet is finished. Then, as at the beginning, a short web end

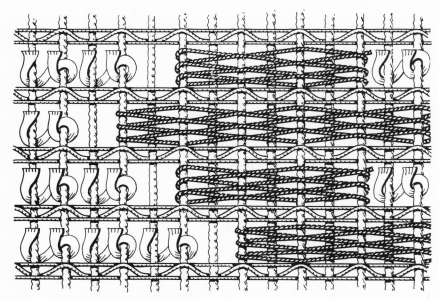

Fig. 38 Knotting and brocading

is formed. Finally, the ends of the warp are usually tied into a fringe, and the pile, having been lightly trimmed after each row, is uniformly clipped (*Fig. 37*).

The number of weft threads, or "shoots," varies. In old Persian carpets, each row of knots might be followed by three shoots, of which the first and the third were tightly stretched and the second left sinuous. Each shoot is usually inserted twice running—i.e., two successive shoots are brought across the same warp thread, so that there are three groups of two, rather than three single shoots. In Indian and Egyptian carpets, these groups may consist of three, or even five, threads. In Anatolian and Caucasian examples we usually find two shoots, one firm and one sinuous; in Spanish carpets each row of knots is followed by several shoots, all of which pass across the same warp thread (*Fig. 41*). If the shoots are firmly drawn and pushed back with the comb, the warp often gives the impression of two separate layers.

One may well wonder, at the sight of some magnificent historic carpet, how long its owner had to wait for it. Half a lifetime, per-

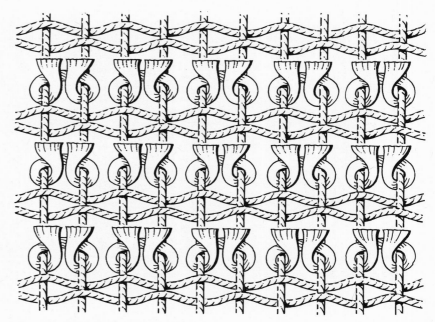

Fig. 39   Ghiordes, or Turkish, knot

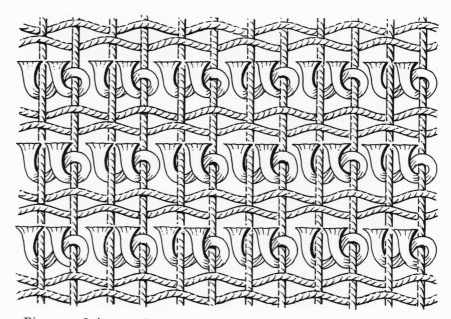

Fig. 40   Sehna, or Persian, knot

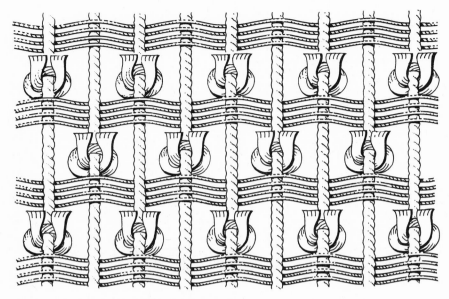

Fig. 41 Spanish, or single-warp, knot

haps, or even more? In a particularly fine example with about 800 knots per square inch and an area of approximately 25 x 11 ft., the total number of knots would be somewhere near 31,680,000. If four weavers worked on the piece, each would have had to produce about 7,920,000 knots. Carpet-weavers have to work fast; a skilled craftsman can make between 8,000 and 12,000 knots per day. If his daily output was 10,000 knots, he would be kept busy for about 792 days. With the additional time needed for inserting the shoots, beating down, strengthening the selvedge and adjusting the loom itself, such a carpet would take about three years.

Tapestry-woven carpets (without pile) were not always considered of little importance in the East—in the golden age of the Persian carpet, woven silk carpets of the highest quality were by no means rare. Today, this type of carpet is made in various sections of the East. In technique it resembles European tapestries (Gobelins and other wall hangings). The pattern-forming thread is inserted between the warp threads, but only as far as the design demands

TAPESTRY-WOVEN CARPETS

271

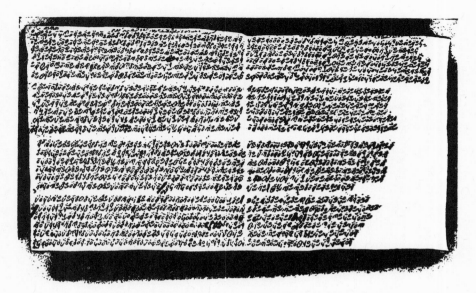

Fig. 42   Instructions to be sung or read out to the weavers at work

Fig. 43   Working drawing

272

(*Fig. 45*). Thus, where the edge of the pattern runs parallel to the warp, slits are formed, since the shoots never pass across the entire width. The weft threads are beaten down so thoroughly that nothing shows of the warp. Today, these smooth-faced tapestry-woven carpets are usually called "kilims" (from *ghilim,* a woven fabric); in the past, they were often known as Karamanies after the town of Karaman in Anatolia. Some Caucasian varieties are known as Silehs and Vernehs (which are made in Shusha).

KILIMS

SILEH, VERNEH

An altogether different technique is used for the so-called Soumaks, whose name is derived from the Caucasian town of Shemakha. The weft thread is brought forward in front of four warp threads and then back behind two. Since the direction of the thread changes in alternate rows, a characteristic herringbone effect is produced. After every—or at least every other—line of stitches, a weft thread, subsequently hidden, is inserted to give strength to the fabric (*Fig. 45*).

SOUMAK

The manufacture of Oriental carpets takes place either in large factories or at home. In the factories, designers are responsible for the pattern and they pay careful attention to the demands of the foreign market. This is evident from the changes in fashion of, for instance, the carpets from Tabriz, Kashan, Kerman, etc.

FACTORIES

Home production may be at a piece rate for an employer who will supply pattern and materials. But nomad tribes and villagers still make the traditional designs, chiefly for their own use. The weavers, in this case, are women. All the materials are obtained from the family flocks. Surplus rugs are sold when the tribe has reached a suitable trading center.

HOME MANUFACTURE

Fig. 44 A wooden comb

Oriental carpets have remained anonymous, the craftsmen and designers completely unknown. No one any longer considers the name Maqsud of Kashan on the Ardebil carpet to refer to the maker. Yet the making of many of the finest carpets in the sixteenth century must have required not merely a design, but also careful teamwork and organization.

DATES   Even dates are not usual. Numerals, apart from small variations, look as follows:

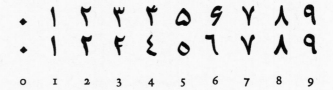

| o | I | 2 | 3 | 4 | 5 | 6 | 7 | 8 | 9 |

To convert Islamic dates to our own, deduct one thirty-third and then add the number 622 (the year Mohammed made his pilgrimage to Mecca). According to this formula, the inscribed date of the Ardebil carpet, 946, is 1539/40.

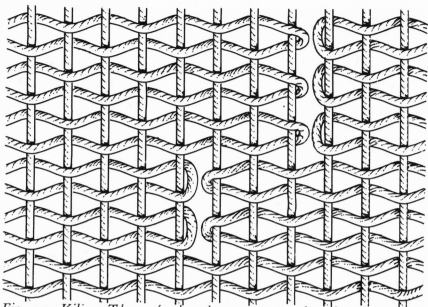

Fig. 45 Kilim: The weft threads pass over and under the warp.

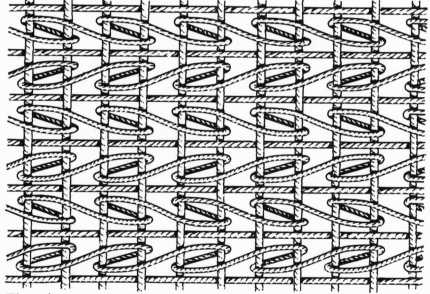

Fig. 46 Soumak: The pattern-forming thread is brought forward
in front of four warp threads and backward behind two, moving
alternately up and down, thus producing a herringbone type of
pattern.

BUYING A CARPET

So-called bargains offered by traveling salesmen, however tempting, should be avoided. The tricks used to deceive the unwary are innumerable, from the gentlemanly caller at the door who, through temporary embarrassment, must dispose cheaply of a valuable piece, to the carpet-vendors who operate by boat, pursuing the tourist until the last moment.

Obviously, Oriental rugs and carpets cannot be cheap, but prices vary and are by no means within reach only of the wealthy. It is possible to pay hundreds of dollars, even thousands, for the finest pieces, but a wide choice is available at more reasonable prices as well. The beginner should go to a reputable dealer, who will give him advice on the type of rug he can buy for the price he is prepared to pay. A dealer will also allow a customer to take pieces home on approval. Above all, he will gladly share his knowledge and will not be angry if no sale results.

Buying at auctions requires some experience, best gained by frequent visits to leading sale rooms. In London, Sotheby's and Christie's as well as other well-known firms hold weekly sales. Goods can generally be inspected daily for nearly a week. In New York, Parke-Bernet Galleries usually have some Oriental rugs and carpets in their Saturday sales, and the Plaza Art Auction Galleries have approximately half a dozen sales devoted exclusively to Oriental rugs every year. Auction catalogues are mines of information. One fact should be kept in mind: Auctioneers accept no responsibility whatever and will not permit a bidder to change his mind after a piece has fallen to him.

The general run of antique shops, as distinct from carpet specialists, should be regarded with caution by the beginner. The average antique-dealer's knowledge of carpets is limited, and although this does undoubtedly make for the occasional bargain, prices may be unrealistic, particularly for very ordinary pieces. The established dealer in Oriental rugs, however, has his reputation to consider and can hardly afford serious mistakes.

DISTINGUISHING BETWEEN HAND-MADE AND MACHINE-MADE

The first step for the beginner is to learn to distinguish between handmade and machine-made carpets. Oriental carpets are invariably made by hand, but this fact does not mean there has been no decline in standards of taste and craftsmanship in the East. On handmade carpets, the fringe is always formed by the warp ends. In the case of machine-made carpets, the fringe is made separately, and the reverse is smooth and even. Many Oriental carpets and rugs of recent years, particularly those made in Teheran, Kashan, Tabriz, and Khurasan, are commercial products with all the characteristic failings of near mass-production: stereotyped designs, colors chosen for their appeal to the Western market—in short, a general effect that is both infinitely monotonous and ostentatious.

In England a floor-covering up to 40 square feet is called a rug; above that size, a carpet. In the United States, the two words are used more or less interchangeably in general practice, though the term "rug" is the one most frequently applied to handmade pieces.

No carpet should be bought without making sure that it will lie really flat. Some have creases or bubbles, or curl at the edges. Creases may result from the way the piece was packed; bubbles, from irregularities in the weave.

BUBBLES, CREASES, AND CROOKEDNESS

Bubbles, creases, and crookedness, which are common in nomad rugs, can be cured or at least reduced by dampening. The rug, having first been thoroughly dampened on the reverse with warm water, should be carefully stretched and nailed to clean boards with very thin nails, and then left to dry.

Colors can be tested by rubbing with a damp cloth. If much color comes off, it is better not to buy that particular piece. Vegetable dyes, provided the carpet is clean and has not been touched up, will not rub off on a damp cloth. Synthetic colors are also fast if they have been used properly; their quality depends on the skill of the dyer. Being much cheaper than vegetable dyes, they have been employed increasingly since the second half of the last century. But where the necessary care was taken in their preparation, they cannot really be considered greatly inferior. Natural dyes are still used for carpets of the highest quality. Riza Shah Pahlavi (1877–1944) even issued a ban against the use of synthetic colors.

Old and antique pieces will usually appear somewhat brighter on the reverse. This may result from dirt on the front surface or from natural fading, which in the case of vegetable dyes and properly used synthetic colors will be comparatively slight.

A liking for dirty and faded colors belongs to the world of brown pictures and stained furniture. Today, the clean, vigorous colors of a rug in its original state seem infinitely preferable. Bleaching, extremely harmful to the fabric, and forced wear are both used to create the impression of age.

The knot count and the type of materials used in warp and weft are also important considerations in buying a carpet. Whether the pile is soft and silky or coarse and brittle can be easily ascertained by feeling. Knots should be counted by the square inch, preferably in several places. Some defects can be seen at a first glance, others only when the carpet is held against the light. Holes or tears, if not too large, can be repaired, and such repairs will not detract greatly from the value of a piece. Repairs in which the warp has to be replaced will show on the back. Very valuable old carpets may have had large, badly damaged, areas cut out, the remaining pieces being joined afterward. This has happened to many of the pieces in museums, without in any way impairing their historical value.

COLOR TEST

FADED COLORS

KNOT COUNT, MATERIALS

REPAIRS

279

Dampness can have serious consequences. It affects the best dyes and causes the warp to rot. Rugs kept rolled up in damp places have often proved beyond repair. Unlike any sound piece, they will not stand up to the simplest tearing test.

Frayed ends and selvedges present no great problem, though they should be repaired as soon as possible if the border is not to suffer. A badly worn pile is hard to replace, though a certain amount of wear is inevitable in older rugs. Expert repairs do not diminish the value of a carpet. There are few older examples that have not been repaired in the course of time.

ANTIQUE, OLD, NEW The trade distinguishes between antique, old, and new. In England, pieces are considered antique, and allowed to be shown at the British Antique Dealers' Fair, if they were made not later than 1830. The term "old" is used more loosely; it now generally covers the period from 1830 to the beginning of World War II. The prospective buyer will have to accept the fact that carpets, like all antiques or works of art, unless dated, are generally credited with a few extra years to make them more interesting. But even dates can be tampered with.

FAKES Fakes of old carpets are extremely rare. The cost, in all probability, would put them out of the reach of all but the wealthiest and most enthusiastic collectors, who are not likely to be deceived.

NAMES A word about names: Unless a buyer intends to build up a collection of certain types, he should buy only carpets he really likes and can use. Names should make little difference. Each village in certain Persian carpet regions may have up to eight hundred looms, and some diversity is therefore inevitable. Designs may also be influenced by adjoining districts, by trade demands, even fashion. Nor can we assume that nomads like the Kashkai tribes, with over 15,000 families, will produce the same designs unchanged year after year. Such a standstill cannot be expected in any popular art. There is, too, a certain amount of competition between tribe and tribe, generation and generation. When a new variation of design appears with

Fig. 47   Traditional arrangement of carpets in a Persian room

281

increasing frequency, the trade will look out for a new name. Thus, many carpets have changed names over the years, and it is therefore impossible to attempt a rigid classification. Changes in old, established patterns have always occurred and will continue to, again and again.

In conclusion, here is a true story which might well apply to carpets: One of the most famous German museum directors had a collection of German Faïence in his care. Here, too, identification is never easy; many pieces bear unknown marks or even none at all, and the situation is further complicated by the extensive travels of most Faïence painters. Whenever experts visited the gallery, they would express an opinion and this was written down and the slip of paper placed into the particular vessel it concerned. After a year, all these "expert" attributions were taken out and studied. Scarcely two of them were ever found to agree.

Therefore, if one has bought, say, a Daghestan, and his more knowledgeable friends give superior smiles, there is no need to feel depressed. The carpet a buyer likes and which suits him does not change with its name.

THE CARE OF CARPETS

In the East, it was the custom to cover floors with carpets from wall to wall. For special occasions, a large and particularly precious carpet was placed in the middle, flanked by two narrow runners of the same length and usually also the same design. A fourth carpet was placed at the top (*Fig.* 47). When such princely solutions were not possible, the floor, whether in nomad tent, private house, or mosque, was covered with smaller pieces.

If these carpets have survived centuries in comparatively good condition, it is because of careful treatment. Only the softest—if any—shoes were worn, and during meals the carpet was protected with hides. What a contrast to the West, where crepe soles, inexpert cleaning, and huge pieces of furniture soon leave their mark. Folding a carpet leads to breaks in warp and weft. In the case of some old pieces, repairs of the more remote past were often primitive in the extreme and did more harm than good.

Next to wear, a carpet's worst enemies are dust, soot, and moths. Dust consists of small, sharp particles that sooner or later will wear through any textile. Moths, left undisturbed, can make large holes, though danger from moths is slight when a carpet is in constant use and is kept free from grease stains. If carpets have to be stored, they should be rolled up and kept in a preferably airtight chest with some paradichlorobenzene crystals, which will have to be

ARRANGEMENT

WEAR

DUST, SOOT, MOTHS

STORAGE

renewed every few months. Ideally, large carpets should be rolled around poles, the protruding ends of which should rest on blocks or trestles. It is not advisable to let carpets lie flat on top of one another for any length of time. Before hanging carpets on the wall one should be certain that the warp threads can stand the strain.

CLEANING

Normally, carpets are either brushed or vacuum-cleaned, always in the direction of—never against—the pile. Older carpets have to be treated with greater care, lest mechanical cleaning affect the pile, though modern vacuum cleaners with special suction attachments are usually safe.

From time to time, a carpet should be cleaned more thoroughly, though not before the colors have been tested for fastness, first with a dry, then a wet, cloth. Often, older pieces have been touched up and therefore will not withstand water.

BEATING

One of the best methods of cleaning is beating, preferably on dry snow, several times on each side. But this is rarely possible in towns. In most cases the carpet will have to be washed. Only the finest

WASHING

soap flakes should be used, the carpet first having been stretched on a clean, firm base. When a solution of the best soap flakes and tepid water has been applied to both sides with a sponge or a very soft brush, it should be rinsed off completely, again on both sides, with softened water. Detergents or chemicals of any kind must not under any circumstances be used. They reduce the fat content, and therefore the luster and durability, of the wool. A very small quantity of wine vinegar added to the last rinse will freshen the colors. Superficial washing cleans only the pile and presses the dirt into the foundation, causing the basic fabric to rot. However, washing as discussed here has nothing to do with chemical "washing," a treatment aimed at making the colors fade and the fabric appear soft, which is thoroughly reprehensible and extremely harmful.

REPAIRS

Repairs should always be carried out by experts. In the case of holes, warp and weft may have to be completely renewed, preferably on the basis of a detailed drawing. Such a task is well beyond even the skilled amateur. Most leading carpet-dealers will supply names of repairers, often outstanding craftsmen in their own right, whose skill has been passed down through many generations.

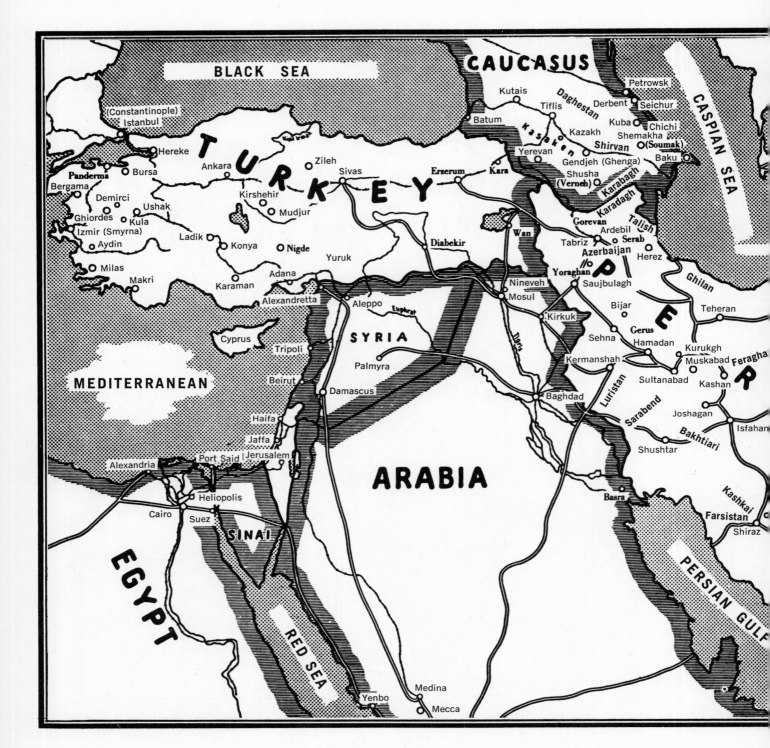

Fig. 48 Carpet trading and manufacturing districts in the East

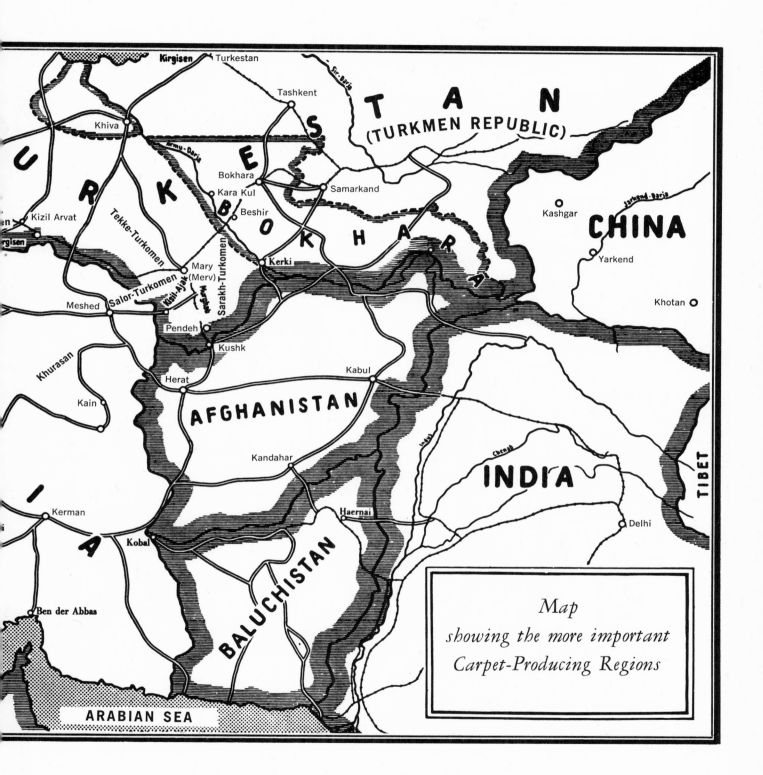

Map
showing the more important
Carpet-Producing Regions

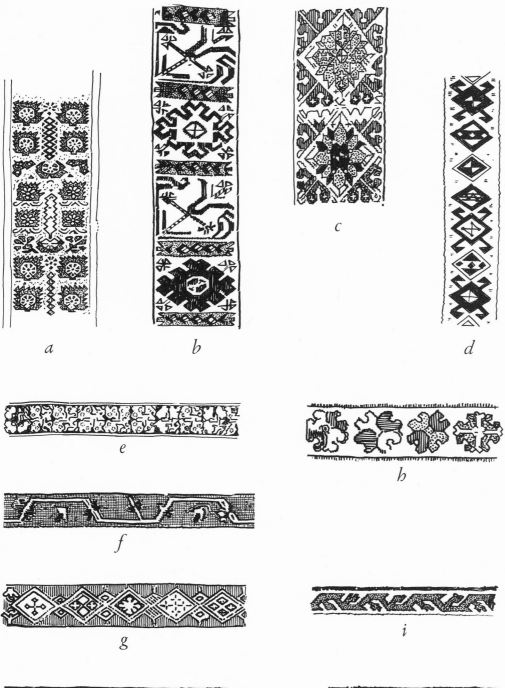

Fig. 49   ANATOLIA (ASIA MINOR)

Borders

a) Ghiordes
b) Ladik
c) Mudjur
d) Yuruk

Guard stripes (secondary border stripes)

e) Ghiordes
f) Ladik
g) Mudjur
h) Milas
i) Anatolian

289

Fig. 50 ANATOLIA (ASIA MINOR)
Cross Panels
a) Ghiordes
b) Tuzla
c) Kirshehir
d) Mudjur
e) Ladik

Spandrels
f) Mudjur
g) Ghiordes

Mihrab
h) Kula (cemetery carpet)
i) Kula
k) Tuzla
l) Milas
m) Makri
n) Kirshehir
o) Ladik

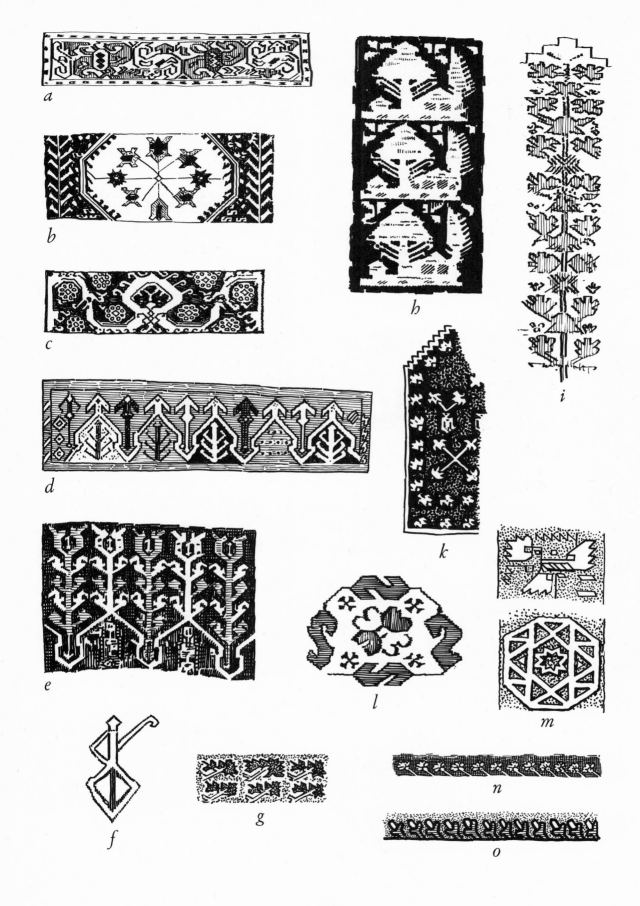

a

b

c

d

e

f

g

h

i

k

l

m

n

o

a

b

c

d

e

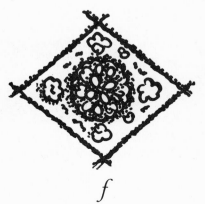

f

Fig. 51   PERSIA
Main border stripes and guard stripes
a) Meshed
b) Tabriz
c) Feraghan
d) Karadagh
e) Joshagan

Rosette
f) Mosul

Fig. 52   PERSIA

All-over patterns

a) Tabriz, *Herati* pattern
b) Karadagh, *Herati* pattern
c) Saujbulagh, *mina khani* pattern
d) Tafrish, Zil-i-Soltan pattern
e) Isfahan, split stem
f) Khurasan, *boteh*
g) Shiraz, *boteh*
h) Tabriz, medallion pendant

293

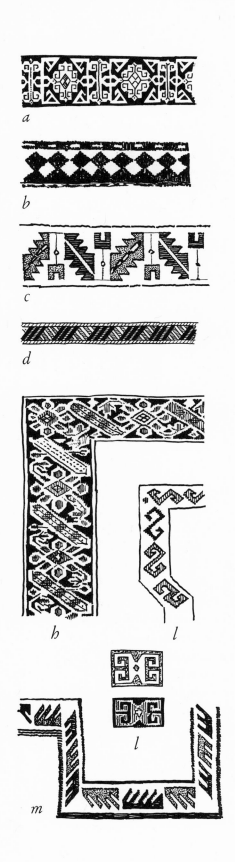

a

b

c

d

h   *l*

l

m

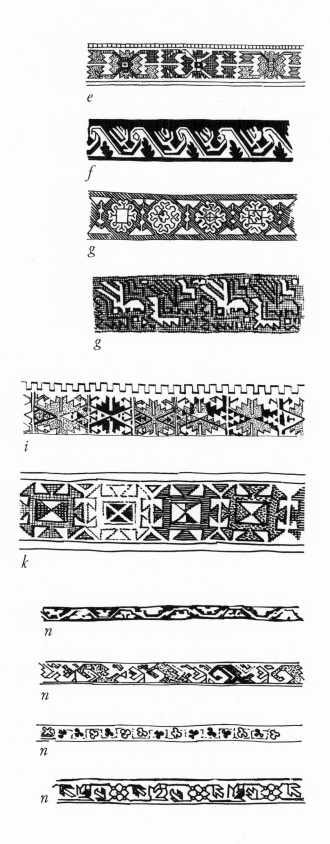

e

f

g

g

i

k

n

n

n

n

Fig. 54 CAUCASUS
Field designs
a) Daghestan
b) Chichi
c) Baku, *boteh*
d) Shemakha
e) Shiraz
f) Derbent, arabesques
g) Kabistan, arabesques

Fig. 55 CAUCASUS

Medallions

a) Kazak (sunburst medallion)
b) Baku
c) Kuba
d) Shemakha
e) Derbent
f) Lezghian
g) Gendjeh (this motif occurs in many types of Caucasian rugs)

297

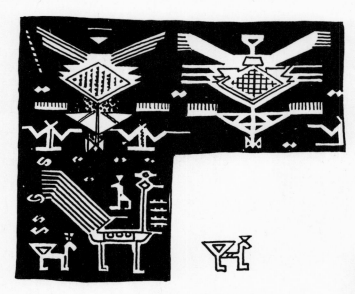
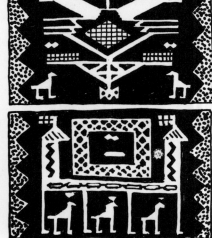

a

b

◁ *Fig. 56* CAUCASUS
Various motifs
a) Verneh
b) Sileh

Fig. 57 TURKESTAN ▷
Main border stripes and guard stripes
a) Yomud
b) Pendeh
c) Tekke
d) Khiva
e) Afghan
f) Samarkand

Field design
g) Yomud, Khatchli

298

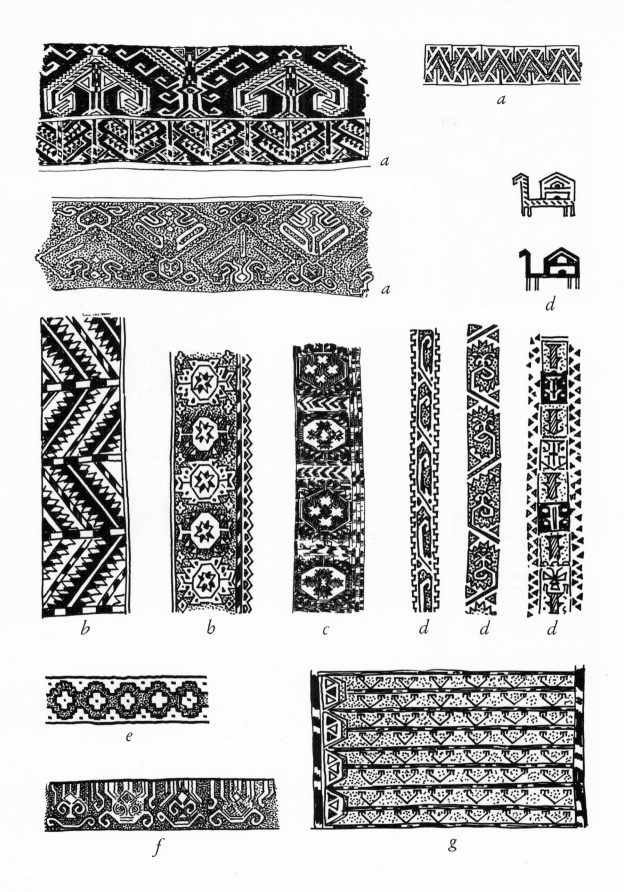

a

a

a

d

b

b

c

d

d

d

e

f

g

Fig. 58 TURKESTAN
Guls
a) Tekke
b) Salor
c) Pendeh
d) Yomud
e) Afghan
f) Baluchi
g) Samarkand

GLOSSARY

ABRASH: Irregularities in the same color, which result when all the wool is not dyed at the same time. This effect is often deliberately produced in machine-made carpets.

ACANTHUS: The well-known acanthus-leaf motif, first used on the Corinthian column, has been repeated ever since throughout the vast orbit of Graeco-Roman culture.

ARABESQUE: A pattern formed of branching tendrils, or stems, with characteristic split leaf-ends. Arabesque and Moresque, both of Eastern origin, have appeared in the decorative arts of Europe since the end of the Middle Ages (*Fig. 4*).

BARBER POLE: A characteristic Shiraz border design of diagonal bands or small lozenge-shaped fields (*Ills. 147, 148*).

BASRAH: A term used for Anatolian rugs with a white ground.

BIRD CARPETS: A type of Anatolian seventeenth-century carpet displaying a pattern of angular leaves on thin stems, vaguely resembling birds.

BLUE BOKHARA: Trade term for Beshir rugs (now little used).

BORDER: The stripes surrounding the field. The width and number of the stripes are to some extent a guide to the date and place of origin of the carpet.

BOTEH: A leaf with a curved tip; also known as the pear, pine cone, and almond patterns (*Figs. 19, 52g, 54c*). In its many variations, the boteh is one of the most common motifs in the decorative arts of the East, being also the principal feature of the Kashmir shawl.

CARTOUCHE: A small, often oddly shaped field which, in European art, generally bears an inscription or heraldic device.

CEMETERY CARPET: A prayer rug with tombs and trees in the mihrab; used in cemeteries and at funerals. These carpets were made in Kula and other places in Asia Minor. The Turkish name is Mazarlek.

CHAIN: The total of the warp threads stretched on the two beams of the loom.

CHI-LIN (*also* KI-LIN): An animal resembling a lion which appears in early Persian art. It is of Chinese origin.

CHINTAMANI: A triangular arrangement of three spheres; of Chinese origin and found in Chinese-influenced carpets. Though a Buddhist symbol, it is also known as the Badge of Timur.

CLOUD BAND: A Chinese motif, widely used in a variety of forms in Persian carpets of the great period (*Figs. 2, 7, 15, 16*).

DRAGONS: The heavily stylized animals in old Caucasian carpets based on Persian examples. For want of any other more accurate name, the term *dragon* is used.

FARS-BAFF: Literally "Persian knots"; e.g., a carpet made with the Persian or Sehna knot (*see* TURK-BAFF).

GARDEN CARPET: A carpet reproducing more or less distinctly the layout of a Persian garden with its camels, pools and flower beds.

GROUND: The principal color.

GUL: A quartered polygon. A type of tribal emblem, the gul is a characteristic feature, and a principal guide to the origin, of Turkoman rugs (*Fig. 58*).

GUL HINNAI: A flower pattern with hyacinth-like blossoms on stiff stems, supposedly representing the henna flower.

HACHLI: The term is sometimes used in place of Khatchli (*which see*).

HERATI: One of the most popular Persian motifs, consisting of a palmette flanked by lanceolate leaves.

HOLBEIN CARPET: A term used for a certain type of Anatolian rug, usually with a pattern of highly stylized yellow arabesques on a red ground—a design not found in any picture by Holbein.

KELLEGHI: Persian. The headpiece in the traditional carpet arrangement of a Persian room.

KENARES: The two narrow carpets at the sides in the traditional Persian arrangement.

KHALI: The principal carpet in the traditional Persian arrangement.

KHATCHLI: Supposedly Armenian for "like a cross." A Turkoman rug marked with a Greek cross, used both as a prayer rug and a tent flap.

KILIM (*also* KELIM): A woven carpet, or the web ends of a knotted carpet.

KIS-GHIORDES: A carpet given to, or woven by, young girls in the East as part of their dowry.

LANCEOLATE LEAF: A narrow curved leaf of saw-edged outline.

LATTICE PATTERN: An arrangement of squares or rectangles giving the impression of latticework (also known as the tile pattern).

LOTUS FLOWER: The lotus flower, originally a very simple motif, appears in infinite variety throughout Asian art.

MADJIDIEH RUGS: These prayer rugs are named after the Sultan Abd-el-Madjid (1839–61). They have a white ground, with patterns clearly influenced by European Second Rococo forms.

MAZARLEK: *see* CEMETERY CARPET.

MEANDER: In the textile arts, a highly stylized, angular version of the scroll or tendril; named after a river in Asia Minor (*Fig. 26*).

MEDALLION: A form of design (there are infinite variations) widely used in all types of rugs, especially in Persian carpets of the Safavid period. A medallion generally appears in the middle of the field, often with one or two pendants.

MIAN FARSH: Persian. The principal carpet in the traditional arrangement of a Persian room.

MIHRAB: The prayer arch in a mosque, or its representation on a carpet.

MINA KHANI: A pattern of rosettes joined by stiff or scrolling stems.

NAMAZLIK: Turkish for prayer rug.

ODJALIK: A rug with a gable at each end of the inner field.

PALMETTE: Originally denoting a specific leaflike form, the term is now widely used to describe a variety of plant motifs.

PILE: The raised surface, silk or wool, of a knotted carpet; the length of the pile varies greatly, depending, apart from the condition of the carpet, on the place of origin.

POLONAISE RUGS: A certain type of seventeenth-century silk rug, often brocaded in gold and silver. The first rugs of this kind to be shown in Europe included some examples bearing the Polish arms, and it was therefore assumed they must have been made in Poland. In the course of time they were clearly established as Persian, though commissioned by the Polish court.

POLYGON: A multisided ornament (*see* GUL).

POMEGRANATE PATTERN: From the end of the Middle Ages, a motif resembling a thistle rather than a pomegranate has appeared in European silk weaving. The name "pomegranate" nevertheless continues to be used.

PORTUGUESE CARPETS: The corners of these carpets show sailing ships with European crews (as on the dust jacket of this volume). Since the Portuguese were the first Europeans in India, these carpets were at first thought to be Indian. The tendency now is to attribute them to Persia.

PRAYER RUG: A rug on which the devout Moslem says his prayers, either kneeling or standing. The principal feature is the mihrab or prayer arch, the design of which varies from place to place.

PRINCESS BOKHARA: Trade term for a Tekke-Turkoman rug with a Khatchli.

RHODOS: Another name for Makri rugs.

ROSETTE: A round, stylized flower with radiating petals (*Figs. 51f and 53e*).

ROYAL BOKHARA: Trade term for Tekke-Turkoman rugs.

ROYAL DAGHESTAN: A name formerly used for rugs from Shemakha, the capital of Shirvan.

RUNNING DOG: A motif of classic origin, frequently found in the arts of the East. It is particularly common in the outer guard stripes of Soumak rugs.

SAPH: So-called family prayer rugs; i.e., rugs with several adjacent mihrabs.

SEDJADEH: A Turkish word meaning "the carpet spread over the seats in front of the divan."

SHAH ABBAS PATTERNS: The patterns of brocaded silk carpets of Persian Court manufacture from the first half of the seventeenth century.

SHOBOKLI: A type of Anatolian border consisting of many stripes. The name is derived from *tchibuk,* the Turkish word for pipe.

SINEKLI: A type of Anatolian rug with a small all-over pattern.

SOUMAK: A woven carpet made with a slightly different technique (described in detail in the chapter "Making a Carpet").

SULTAN: Name occasionally used for Kirshehir rugs.

TORBA: A small Turkoman tent bag.

TRANSYLVANIAN RUGS: From 1526 to 1699, Transylvania was under Turkish rule, but the interest in carpets, strong even before the occupation, continued, and many fine examples have survived, particularly in churches. A certain type of Anatolian rug, usually with a mihrab at each end, vases or naturalistic flowers in the field, and a border of polygons and arabesques, has come to be known as Transylvanian.

TURK-BAFF: A carpet made in the Turkish manner; i.e., with the Ghiordes knot.

VASE CARPET: Carpets of a rich floral design which usually—but by no means always—includes a vase.

ZIL-I-SOLTAN: A vase pattern named after a Quajar prince who was governor of Isfahan at the end of the last century.

BIBLIOGRAPHY

ANTHONY, E. A. *A History of Mosaic,* Boston, 1935

ARSEVEN, C. E. *Les arts décoratifs turcs,* Istanbul, 1950

BERNHEIMER, O. *Alte Teppiche*

BODE, W. VON. *Altorientalische Tierteppiche,* Vienna, 1892

——. *Altpersische Knüpfteppiche,* Berlin, 1904

BODE, W. V., and KÜHNEL, E. *Vorderasiatische Knüpfteppiche aus alter Zeit,* Brunswick, 1955. Also published in an English edition, *Antique Rugs from the Near East,* transl. by C. G. Ellis, Brunswick, 1955

CAMPANA, M. *Il tappeto orientale,* Milan, 1945

CLARK, H. *Bokhara, Turkoman and Afghan Rugs,* London, 1922

DIEZ, E. *Die Kunst der islamischen Völker, Handbuch der Kunstwissenschaft,* Berlin, 1917

DILLEY, A. U. *Oriental Rugs and Carpets,* New York, 1931

DIMAND, M. S. *A Handbook of Mohammedan Decorative Arts,* New York, 1930

DUNN, E. *Rugs in Their Native Lands,* London, 1910

EDWARDS, A. CECIL. *The Persian Carpet,* London, 1953

ELLWANGER, W. D. *The Oriental Rug,* New York, 1906

ERDMANN, K. *Der orientalische Knüpfteppich,* Tübingen, 1956

——. *Der türkische Teppich des 15. Jahrhunderts*

FARADAY, C. B. *European and American Carpets and Rugs,* Michigan, 1929

GLÜCK, H. and DIEZ, E. *Die Kunst des Islam, Propyläen Kunstgeschichte,* Vol. V, 1925

GROTE-HASENBALG, W. *Der Orientteppich, seine Geschichte und seine Kultur,* Berlin, 1922

HAWLEY, W. A. *Oriental Rugs, Antique and Modern.* New York, 1913

HEINZ, D. *Alte Orientteppiche,* 1956

HILDEBRAND, H. *Der persische Teppich und seine Heimat,* Zürich, 1951

HOLT, R. B. *Rugs, Oriental and Occidental,* Chicago, 1901

JACOBY, H. *How to Know Oriental Carpets and Rugs,* London, 1952

KENDRICK, A. F. *Notes on Carpet Knotting and Weaving,* London, 1920

KENDRICK, A. F., and TATTERSALL, C. E. C. *Handwoven Carpets, Oriental and European*, 2 vols., London, 1922

――――. *Fine Carpets in the Victoria and Albert Museum*, London, 1922

KOECHLIN, R., and MIGEON, G. *Islamische Kunstwerke*, Berlin, 1928

KÜHNEL, E. *Maurische Kunst*, Berlin, 1924

KÜHNEL, E., and BELLINGER, L. *Catalogue of Spanish Rugs, 12th-19th Centuries*, Textile Museum, Washington, D.C., 1953

――――. *Catalogue of Cairene Rugs and Others Technically Related*, Textile Museum, Washington, D.C., 1955

KULCZYCKI, W. *Beiträge zur Kenntnis des orientalischen Gebetsteppichs*, Lemberg (Lvov), 1914

LEWIS, G. G. *The Practical Book of Oriental Rugs*, Philadelphia, 1920

MARTIN, F. R. *A History of Oriental Carpets before 1800*, Vienna, 1908

MAZZINI, F. *Tappeti orientali*, Livorno, 1947

MIGEON, G. *Manuel d'art Musulman*, Paris, 1927

MUMFORD, J. K. *Oriental Rugs*, New York, 1901

MUSTAFA, M. *Turkish Prayer Rugs*, Cairo, 1953

NEUGEBAUER, R., and TROLL, S. *Handbuch der orientalischen Teppich-kunde*, Leipzig, 1930

ORENDI, J. *Das Gesamtwissen über antike und neue Teppiche des Orients*, Vienna, 1930

ÖTTINGEN, R. v. *Meisterstücke orientalischer Knüpfkunst*, Berlin, 1912

POPE, A. U. *Survey of Persian Art*, London, 1931

RIEGL, A. *Orientalische Teppiche*, Vienna, 1892-1895

RIPLEY, M. C. *The Oriental Rug Book*, New York, 1904

ROPERS, H. *Morgenländische Teppiche*, Brunswick, 1953

SARRE, F. *Altorientalische Teppiche*, Leipzig, 1908

SARRE, F., and MARTIN, F. R. *Die Ausstellung von Meisterwerken muhammedanischer Kunst in München*, 1910

SARRE, F., and TRENKWALD, H. *Altorientalische Teppiche*. English edition, *Old Oriental Carpets*, transl. by A. F. Kendrick; 2 vols., Vienna and Leipzig, 1926

SCHMUTZLER, E. *Altorientalische Teppiche in Siebenbürgen*, Leipzig, 1932

STEIN, SIR A., *Ancient Khotan*, Oxford, 1907

――――. *Serindia*, Oxford, 1921

――――. *Innermost Asia*, Oxford, 1926

STERNER, MAJ. *Orientens mattor och deras vard*, Stockholm, 1944

TATTERSALL, C. E. C. *The Carpets of Persia*, London, 1931

――――. *A History of British Carpets*, London, 1934

TROLLS, S. *Altorientalische Teppiche*, Vienna, 1951

UHLEMANN, H. *Geographie des Orientteppichs*, Leipzig, 1930

WESTERMANN, *Aegte Taepper*, Copenhagen, 1942

Numerous articles in the following periodicals:
Apollo
Ars Islamica
Artibus Asiae
Belvedere
Berliner Museen
Bulletin of the Metropolitan Museum
Burlington Magazine
Cicerone
Dedalo
Gazette des Beaux Arts
Jahrbuch der preussischen Kunstsammlungen
Kunstchronik
Kunstwanderer
Kunstwelt
Kunst und Kunsthandwerk
Ostasiatische Zeitschrift
The Art Bulletin
Zeitschrift für bildende Kunst

FAMOUS MUSEUM COLLECTIONS

Berlin: Staatliche Museen, Islamic Section
Boston: Museum of Fine Arts
Cairo: Museum of Islamic Art
Hamburg: Museum für Kunst und Gewerbe
Istanbul: Türk ve Islam Eserleri Müzesi
London: Victoria and Albert Museum
Lyon: Musée historique des tissus
Milan: Museo Poldi-Pezzoli
Munich: Residenzmuseum
————: Staatliche Völkerkunde Museum
New York: Hispanic Society of America
————: Metropolitan Museum of Art
Paris: Musée des arts décoratifs
————: Musée des Gobelins
————: Musée du Louvre
Philadelphia: Museum of Art
Vienna: Österreichisches Museum für angewandte Kunst
Washington, D.C.: Corcoran Art Gallery
————. Textile Museum

SOURCES OF ILLUSTRATIONS

INDEX

Italic entries refer to illustrations.